PREP

REP

REPEAT

FROM AVERAGE TO IRON

Bradley Barmore

simply francis publishing company
North Carolina

Library of Congress Control Number: 2024926323
ISBN: 978-1-63062-064-6 (paperback)
ISBN: 978-1-63062-065-3 (e-book)
Printed in the United States of America
Front Cover-*Barmore Photo Collection*
Cover and Interior Design: Christy King Meares

For information about this title or to order books and/or electronic media, contact the publisher:

simply francis publishing company
P.O. Box 329, Wrightsville Beach, NC 28480
www.simplyfrancispublishing.com
simplyfrancispublishing@gmail.com

Approximately 97% of books in this world are unfinished. I won't let mine become a part of that statistic.

DEDICATION

To my wife Adrienne, and my sons, Beckett and Rush: You have filled my life with more joy than I could have ever imagined. You have been, and continue to be, my greatest inspiration in pursuing life's most ambitious endeavors.

TABLE OF CONTENTS

PREFACE

I started writing this book on a Tuesday night, with the support of my wife, Adrienne, and my son, Beckett. Adrienne offered valuable insights, while Beckett contributed a blue crayon, which he later swapped for a red one. Before you turn the page, I want to make it clear that this book might not be the magical solution you've been seeking. You won't read it and instantly achieve your ideal goals. Even if you read it a thousand times, without taking action after reaching the last page, it's just another plan.

Now that we've established that, let me explain why I'm writing a book about the pursuit of an Iron Life. What exactly is an Iron Life? Let's back up even further, what is an Ironman?

An Ironman is a formidable triathlon that includes a 2.4 mile swim, a 112 mile bike ride, and concludes with a 26.2 mile run/walk. This challenge seemed far beyond my grasp, a daunting feat that felt almost unreal. In the following pages, I will share the reasons behind my fascination with the extraordinary goal and what drove me to pursue it with relentless action and unlimited hope.

First, let's explore the Iron Life that we all secretly yearn for. It's the life we envision and dream of—a life where we realize our true potential and strive for greatness. It involves giving your all in everything you do from morning until night. Unfortunately, very few of us actually reach that point of fulfillment; many of us create narratives that life is unfair or that we are too busy to succeed. We might feel "too far off course" or think "this is all I will ever be." Have you ever encountered those thoughts? Even better, have you ever found yourself repeating those untruths? I have too!

That is exactly why I'm writing this book. I once thought I had reached the highest point of what I could achieve in my life. I never imagined myself running a marathon, let alone completing a full Ironman. I didn't believe I would ever pick up a book again after college, nor did I ever think I could make six figures in a single year. It was all about doubt, doubt, doubt, and disbelief.

We are conditioned—no, we are programmed—to think that we must stay within the boundaries of our environment and that we aren't deserving of exceeding those limits. We're often told what we can expect to become in life, and we ultimately accept those limitations. This book aims to empower you to eliminate the belief in limitations and transform your ordinary life into the Iron Life you desire.

We are about to embark on a journey through a collection of my personal concepts and theories, drawn from my experiences in life, coaching, teaching, and my journey as an Ironman athlete. Before you begin this transformation, it is essential to embrace an open mind. Allow yourself the freedom to think beyond conventional boundaries. Many exceptionally talented individuals remain uncharted because they resist seeking guidance. Ultimately, you hold the power to determine the influence this book and your life's experiences will have on your future. Now is the moment to break free from old patterns and initiate meaningful change.

Martin Luther King, Jr. once remarked, "Change does not

roll in on the wheels of inevitability, but comes through continuous struggle." Change will happen regardless of our willingness to accept it. Nonetheless, growth is not assured; as King wisely noted, it will never "roll in on the wheels of inevitability." To truly grow, you must first desire it. You need to actively pursue it, being intentional and purposeful in every action you take.

INTRODUCTION

Like any fundamental aspect of life, one of the most challenging phases is the stage of acceptance and initiation. Too often, individuals engage in endless discussion without taking decisive action; their words outpace their ability to act. Why does this happen?

While there may not be a singular definition for this phenomenon, I will delve into the essence of my "Prep-Rep-Repeat" philosophy. This system not only prepared me for my Ironman journey but also lifted me from the depths of adversity, guiding me toward a fulfilling life—an Iron Life. It has opened avenues of opportunity I once thought were beyond my reach. My deepest hope is that it will similarly empower you to transform your aspirations into tangible realities.

This is not merely a concept. It is a comprehensive blueprint designed to cultivate the discipline and focus necessary to mold the life you envision. This framework can enhance various facets of your existence, including fitness, relationships, financial objectives, and any other key areas of your life. Many successful individuals have effectively adopted a variation of the Prep-Rep-Repeat mentality. Are you feeling the anticipation yet? BRAD! What exactly is Prep-Rep-Repeat? I'll address that shortly, but first, allow me to introduce myself properly and share a glimpse into my personal journey.

My name is Bradley Barmore. I do not consider myself an

1

author—at least I didn't, until the publication of this book. I am not an elite figure in any particular domain. I am an ordinary individual who has translated my thoughts into actionable steps. I held a vision and committed to pursuing it. While I will elaborate on my wife, Adrienne, and my sons, Beckett and Rush, later in this narrative, it feels essential to acknowledge them at the outset. They are my foundation, and without their support, I would not have mustered the courage to write this book or to pursue any of my dreams. I love you all dearly!

We are now ready to embark on this journey! Let's take a moment to reflect on my teenage years, particularly the time when I graduated high school. At the age of eighteen, the world appeared to be full of possibilities. It was 2006, and I was at my graduation party at my parents' home, enjoying cake and sipping grape soda while mingling with friends, family, and former coaches.

When I approached one of my high school hockey coaches, he posed a question that, while simple, carried significant weight. What did I envision for my future? I contemplated this for a brief moment, confident I knew the answer. I expressed my aspiration to elevate my game and play college hockey. Initially, my coach responded with an odd smile, setting his plate down, and looking me directly in the eyes. I anticipated an encouraging speech or supportive words.

Instead, his response pierced my heart. He told me it was time to mature and transition from dreaming to facing reality.

"Brad," he said, "you should really focus on something meaningful. It's time to stop playing games."

In 2007, I gave up on my dream of playing next level hockey because I let the words of others sink in and disturb my vision of pursuing greater things. To this day, I think about the "what if" but I've learned to use that to my advantage. Never again will I leave something on the table because of external influence.
Barmore Photo Collection

3

In that instant, I could have reacted in myriad ways, but I chose to trust him. More troubling was the fact that I believed him. He was a figure I respected greatly—someone I admired and valued. At that moment, I ceased to dream. I abandoned nearly all of my aspirations, convinced by his words that "the next level" was reserved for the elite, for the exceptional, and that I was not among them. The respect I held for him as a coach and leader made it difficult to dismiss his advice.

By laughing at my dreams, he inadvertently conveyed that I wasn't even worthy of attempting to pursue them. It would take me years to realize that my goal was never too grand for me, it was merely too expansive for his limited perspective. Unfortunately, I did not recognize this truth until much later, and I never pursued my ambition of playing hockey at a higher level.

When asked why I didn't try, I crafted every possible excuse—I was in love, I didn't want to leave my family, and the offers on the table weren't adequate. I could recount a thousand excuses, but they ultimately stemmed from one reality: I was surrounded by people who thought too small, unable to envision what I aspired to achieve in hockey.

There are instances when dreams are belittled by others, not because they doubt you, but rather because they fear being surpassed. Reflect on the last time you confided a challenging goal to a loved one. Their initial smile may have dissolved into skepticism, accompanied by questions like "Why" or "I don't think you should."

It's disheartening, but those closest to us can sometimes lead us towards irrational decisions that don't serve our best interests. I firmly believe that we become reflections of those we surround ourselves with.

A quote that has resonated with me over the years states, "If you want to be a millionaire, surround yourself with four millionaires, and you'll become the fifth. If you want to be a 'bum,' associate with four bums, and you'll become the fifth."

This was my reality! I was enveloped by individuals who were mentally bankrupt, incapable of imagining a small-town kid achieving greater things, let alone reaching the next level. Without a plan or guidance, my direction became obscured, and I felt lost for much of my twenties. In search of fleeting highs on Friday nights, I turned to alcohol for comfort, anticipating the weekend with eagerness. I found solace in that immediate gratification, unaware that I was grappling with alcohol abuse.

My evenings would often consist of coming home from school or work to indulge in beers, concluding the night with bourbon. I had descended into one of the darkest periods of my life. This behavior was not confined to a couple of nights a week; it spanned five to seven nights.

This cycle inevitably led to more poor choices—drinking and driving, indulging in fast food, engaging in conflicts with loved ones, and so much more. Each word I pen evokes sadness as I relive these nightmares. I was on a destructive trajectory with no discernible destination. I had effectively set my life on cruise control, merely existing. While from the outside, others offered lifelines to assist me, I was unwilling to be saved.

As a few years passed, I approached the conclusion of my college journey when I met Adrienne. She became the beacon of hope I desperately needed in my life. Having recently returned from Miami, Florida, Adrienne was committed to personal growth and living an optimal existence. The irony was that she crossed paths with me—a young man spiraling into an abyss. Remember the saying? You become who you surround yourself with, and I was taking this youthful, ambitious woman and weighing her down with my negativity.

Initially, neither of us recognized the significance of what was happening in our new relationship. We mistakenly believed we were "living the dream." The mantra of YOLO, "You Only Live Once" was a highlight for a period when I was in college, and we thought we were living the YOLO lifestyle. How wrong were we? How wrong I was!

I had taken a goal-oriented, hardworking, driven young woman and killed her ambition. Gradually, Adrienne regressed, drifting further away from the vibrant person I had initially met. Month by month, year by year, we descended deeper into a state of stagnation, sinking into increasingly darker corners, devoid of any real plans to reclaim our lives.

We married, purchased a home, and settled into stable jobs. At this juncture, I mistakenly believed I had life figured out. From an outsider's perspective, it may have appeared that we were doing well—and while it was true that we were "fine," we both deserved so much more than that. In the waning days of my twenties, I found myself approaching rock bottom, but Adrienne was not. She sensed her own free fall and recognized that it was time to dig her heels in and start climbing.

I was entrenched in my teaching career at Sherman Central School, a small institution in Western New York, while Adrienne was working for a clothing enterprise and increasingly traveling for work. Our relationship began to shift.

"Thank God! Brad has finally figured it out. He's reached a pivotal moment and is going to turn his life around," people remarked.

This assumption couldn't have been more misguided. In truth, it was Adrienne who had begun to reinvent her life.

Surrounded by a diverse array of cultured colleagues from around the globe, she encountered individuals who spoke multiple languages, embraced health and fitness, and actively sought to maximize their potential. They were engaged in noteworthy pursuits, and she was captivated by their stories.

She returned home from her travels brimming with excitement and eager to share the remarkable people she had met. As she recounted these conversations, I often found myself tuning out, overwhelmed by the stark contrast between their dynamic lives and my own stagnation. With each trip and each enriching conversation, we drifted farther apart. Adrienne reignited her zest for life and rediscovered her eagerness to grow—attributes that should have served as the impetus for my own transformation.

Instead of harnessing her newfound motivation to propel me forward, I judged her for seeking change. Adrienne was evolving, rediscovering the woman she had been before we met. Rather than supporting her, I felt threatened by her ascent, anchored as I was by feelings of inadequacy. Our relationship became a tumultuous rollercoaster ride over the course of nearly five years, as she attempted to broaden my perspective while I sought to confine her to the familiar life we had shared.

Each time she returned from a trip, filled with inspiration and excitement, I inadvertently stifled her enthusiasm and attention. In truth, I was oblivious to the concept of dreaming, lacking even the faintest understanding of what it meant to have an appetite for growth. I am going to pause here for now, as I plan to delve deeper into this topic in the upcoming chapters.

Why do I share this chapter of my life in the introduction?

When we think of individuals who have achieved anything

close to greatness, we often perceive them as flawless. One of my most valuable qualities today is my ability to be honest and transparent with my friends, family, and now my readers. I am by no means perfect. I possess numerous voids in my life. The reality is that we all have our shortcomings, yet I refuse to spend another day without striving to address each and every one of them, no matter how long the journey may take. There is always room for improvement. Do not confine yourself with a fixed mindset. Embrace the potential for growth, remain open to learning, and enjoy the journey!

CHAPTER 1

THE OUTBREAK

March 2020 was undoubtedly an unusual period in history. The outbreak of COVID-19 forced students and faculty at Sherman Central School to transition to remote learning, effectively upending our traditional teaching practices. This unprecedented shift caught my colleagues and me off guard, plunging us into a landscape fraught with uncertainty.

Many aspects of my life that I had come to regard as staples were abruptly stripped away before my eyes. The cancellation of baseball and football for that year was particularly disheartening. Having umpired baseball for two decades, I had developed a profound passion for being on the diamond. My journey began at the age of thirteen, inspired by the men in blue at our local professional team, the Jamestown Jammers. By 2020, my experience spanned little league, high school, college, and even some professional ball, culminating in the remarkable opportunity to officiate a 13-Year-Old World Series. The game of baseball imparted invaluable life lessons, and its absence left me feeling as though I had lost a crucial part of myself.

Additionally, I was approaching my tenth year of coaching high school football. As the news broke that the fall season might be canceled, anxiety crept in. Overwhelmed by uncertainty, I immediately shared the news with Adrienne. It is in years like 2020, that individuals are either shaped or shattered. This year was instrumental in defining who I am today.

While I do not wish to trivialize the suffering experienced by millions during this time, I view it as the awakening I desperately needed. It was during this period that I realized life was not simply a matter of fight or flight; it was fundamentally about fighting for what I wanted and for my future. Clarity struck me like a lightning bolt, illuminating opportunities that had long been present, yet overlooked. I began to recognize the potential laid before me, although realizing my goals still required several strategic moves.

I am someone who thrives on structure and routine. Downtime does not sit well with me, so when my baseball season was canceled, I knew I needed a contingency plan. Social gatherings, which I typically cherished, were suddenly off the table.

In response, I turned to my ATV club, Herby's Mud Club, composed of some of my closest friends. We gathered on 300 acres in Gerry, New York, where we reveled in navigating the thickest mud imaginable—deeper than what you might envision, and certainly thicker. It was a haven off the beaten path where we could safely practice social distancing, allowing us to convene almost every Friday. As I became increasingly immersed in the world of ATVs, I began capturing video content on my iPhone and uploading it to our Instagram.

This endeavor was purely for enjoyment until I received an outreach from a company called Finntrail. Renowned within the off-road industry, Finntrail was known for endorsing only those deemed worthy. This unexpected recognition was astonishing and served as a catalyst, showcasing that significant accomplishments can arise when one fully invests in a pursuit. Through this experience, I learned that persistence is the universal key capable of unlocking new opportunities.

As summer rolled in and the reality of no football season loomed alongside the impending conclusion of our ATV season, I found myself almost back at square one, needing a new outlet. It was during this time that my brother-in-law, Nick Jackson, introduced me to the world of podcasts. Although I had always been aware of their existence, I had never taken the time to appreciate their potential value. This perspective shifted dramatically upon listening to Andy Frisella's "MFCEO Project."

From the moment I hit play, I was confronted with unabashed language and raw authenticity that resonated deeply with my own experiences. While Frisella's delivery was as colorful as it was unfiltered, I found relatable insights within his exuberance. This podcast became the spark I needed to transition from a state of inertia to one of proactive engagement.

Oftentimes, it is the manner in which a message is conveyed or the identity of the messenger that ignites the necessary motivation to invigorate change. One day in September, after a long drive home from school, I vividly remember sharing with Adrienne the insights from a podcast centered on leveraging hardship and adversity to fuel personal growth. The speaker emphasized the importance of transforming losses into learning opportunities.

Adrienne's reaction was immediate and visceral. Her face fell in disbelief as I chuckled, sensing what might be coming

11

next. She calmly—but not entirely calmly—replied, "I've been telling you this for seven years," and then walked away.

It felt as though a thousand revelations detonated in my mind. I realized I had been hearing her words but failing to absorb their significance. Emotion washed over me as I recalled all the times she had extended her support, leading to a moment of profound self-reflection. I experienced a sensation akin to a "Scrooge" moment, momentarily revisiting all the wake-up calls she had offered. Was I truly that lost? Had I been so entrenched in my own confusion that I couldn't grasp the wisdom my wife had been imparting?

At thirty-two-years old, married, in a stable job with a son, I had inappropriately convinced myself that I had life figured out. That day marked a critical moment of reckoning. When I ascended the stairs toward an upset wife, I consoled her and acknowledged it was time to change. Standing in front of the bathroom mirror, I looked into my own eyes and declared, "This isn't enough. You are not enough."

Confronting oneself with brutal honesty is a daunting endeavor, but at that moment, I understood the necessity of holding myself to a higher standard. Did I genuinely wish to continue coasting through life on autopilot, relinquishing my future to chance? Did I want to labor for thirty years, only to retire with an uncertain pension? Did I aspire to merely wish, hope, and dream regarding my health and fitness? Was I content to wake up each morning next to the woman I love, only to express my affection without the corresponding action?

Words, while powerful, often fall short without substantive follow-through. That was the day I resolved to synchronize my actions with my aspirations. I acknowledged that it was time to take decisive action rather than merely talking about what I intended to achieve. Surprisingly, this choice became abundantly clear. To this day, I reflect on why transformation took so long, but I understand that life is composed of various seasons, each playing a crucial role in shaping who we are. Embrace each phase with gratitude while remaining open to growth and expansion.

The individuals in my life who had been encouraging me finally galvanized my momentum, and September marked the moment of action. I sensed that I had a meaningful gift—a superpower, if you will—and it was time to leverage it effectively.

My desire to connect with others, inspire change, and motivate individuals took center stage. Several of my high school student-athletes reached out for fitness advice and encouragement, but I struggled with how to impart my knowledge while ensuring their safety amid ongoing social distancing measures.

Coaching had always been a passion of mine; I cherished the connections with the athletes, the life lessons shared, the camaraderie fostered, and the thrills of road trips under Friday night lights. The absence of football left me feeling as though my platform for motivation and teaching was fading, much like the sounds of a small-town Friday night echoing into silence. The momentum I had built in August seemed to dwindle away.

In light of this, I reached out to a close friend, Jeff Witherspoon. More than just a friend, Jeff is family—our resemblance is evident in any photograph we share. He is the founder of E2M Personal Training, a successful weight loss company that epitomized what I aspired to achieve. I held him in high regard, both professionally and personally. Having established a virtual fitness empire, I knew he could provide the guidance I sought.

I confided in Jeff about the lull I was experiencing and expressed my desire to formalize my work with young athletes by obtaining a personal training certification. My goal was to inspire and transform lives in the same manner that he had been doing through E2M.

At that time, I was training approximately ten young athletes, aged fourteen to eighteen, and I was not seeking a job or overnight success in the fitness industry. I simply wanted the credentials to support my athletes during a time when their sports seasons had been stripped away.

Jeff responded almost immediately, presenting me with an opportunity that would alter the trajectory of my life. He mentioned that he was looking to hire a male personal trainer for his business and asked if I would be interested. Naturally, I was eager to seize the chance. For the first time in my adult life, I made the conscious decision to pause before reacting. I reminded myself to slow down, breathe, and reflect. I was overwhelmed—giddy, anxious, nervous, and excited all at once. The impulse to reply with an enthusiastic "YES, OF COURSE I WILL JOIN" was strong, but I chose to discuss the opportunity with my wife first.

In our relationship, I often serve as the accelerator while Adrienne plays the role of the brake, having steered me away from numerous impulsive decisions. We engaged in a thoughtful conversation, and to my delight, she matched my enthusiasm, exclaiming, "YES, YES, YES, OF COURSE YOU SHOULD."

With that said, I realized that balancing two jobs alongside my responsibilities as a husband, father, and individual seeking joy would be challenging. When unique opportunities arise, immediate decisions can be perilous. Thus, I employed the 3-6-9 rule. This rule prompts reflection on how a decision made today will affect me three, six, and nine days, weeks, months, or even years down the line.

That same evening, I messaged Jeff to express my eagerness to join his team. By fall, I had successfully earned my ISSA Personal Training certification after several weeks of coursework, preparing me for the next phase of my journey. Although it took time before I could lead my first class, Jeff later reached out, asking if I could fill in for him that December. It was at this moment that my true story began—this was when I discovered the principles of Prep-Rep-Repeat and learned how to apply them to not only fitness but to every aspect of my life.

Part 1
PREP

CHAPTER 2

YOUR PEOPLE

Exposure is essential—your growth is directly proportional to the level of exposure you attain. Reflect on the individuals within your immediate circle. When you encounter those who are genuinely invested in helping you become your best self, it is imperative to harness that energy and maintain their presence in your life, as such people are rare. Intentionally cultivate a network of like-minded individuals who share your aspirations. They will propel you to heights you never thought possible.

If your goal is to excel in running, immerse yourself in the community of runners. If you aim to thrive in climbing, connect with climbers and immerse yourself within those specialized communities. While this may seem straightforward, far too many individuals continue to spend time with friends who are content to lounge around a campfire, indulging in cheese puffs, downing light beer, or watching The Wheel of Fortune.

I recognize that this observation may come across as condescending, and you might think I am perched atop a high horse. Yet, I speak from personal experience—this was once my reality. I empathize with the seemingly endless cycle of habits that can feel insurmountable to escape. For too long, I was imprisoned by my own choices: consuming excessive amounts of light beer, ordering pizza or fast-food multiple nights a week, binging on reruns of reality television, and uttering phrases like, "It must be nice to have a house like that," or "I wish I could catch a break."

It all begins innocently enough with Thirsty Thursdays, leading into Friday nights with friends and Saturday night festivities, all topped off with the obligatory Sunday Funday. This vicious cycle becomes increasingly difficult to break free from, especially when surrounded by those unwilling to change their patterns.

At some point, you must confront yourself in the mirror and engage in a candid self-assessment. Seriously consider what you aspire to become and scrutinize your circle of support. Does your current network align with the narrative of who you want to be? If the answer is no, it may be time to create distance between yourself and your so-called "friends." Remaining in close proximity to toxic individuals will only lead you to a place I refer to as "Nowheresville," a purgatory where dreams are extinguished and aspirations are crushed.

A quote that resonated with me profoundly, akin to the electrifying riffs of Slash during a performance of "West Coast Struttin'," declares, "Change your friends or change your yourself."

This statement, deceptively simple yet deeply insightful, underscores the importance of aligning yourself with those who match your ambitions. If your current circle is unwilling to ascend to where you aspire to go, it may be time to reassess those you choose to surround yourself with.

Accompanied by the people that inspired me professionally.
Barmore Photo Collection

I found myself newly immersed in the "growth mindset," surrounded by the inspiring trainers at E2M. Whitney, Mandy, Alicia, Jamie, and the company's owner, Jeff, were all driven by goals and dreams, and they were individuals who truly followed through on their intentions. They were not merely talkers. Their actions spoke volumes about their commitments and aspirations. They epitomized the essence of execution.

Having never previously been in a circle like this, I experienced both fear and exhilaration. It was a thrilling prospect, albeit daunting, because their fervor was entirely foreign to me. I had never considered many of the pursuits they undertook, nor had I traveled, communicated, or moved in the ways they did. They possessed something extraordinary, and from the moment I began interacting with this group, I felt a spark of enlightenment. Simply being in their orbit inspired me to elevate my own ambitions.

One of my colleagues during this transformative time, Jamie Touchberry, was a triathlete. At the time, I had limited knowledge about the triathlon world, but I was on the verge of opening my mind and body to a completely new experience. While I was unfamiliar with the specifics of what an Ironman entailed, Jamie piqued my curiosity, particularly after she completed an Ironman in Cambridge, Maryland, in September of 2021. Her insights into this formidable challenge captivated me.

She detailed the intricate components of swimming, biking, and running—fortitude, resilience, preparation, and everything in between. Though I was a mere novice in this realm, I craved that experience. "Find something you fear and chase it." A mantra I use to conclude every workout, gathering, or speaking engagement emphasizes this principle. When I declare, "If you fear it," the crowd responds in unison, "CHASE IT!" This reinforces the notion that fear should propel you forward. Embrace it, as you will never know the potential outcomes if you do not attempt it.

I was ready to embark on this remarkable journey, thanks to Jamie and although I had little experience in the triathlon scene and was uncertain of what lay ahead, I felt a compelling urge to face the challenge. With a mix of excitement and nerves, I typed "Ironman Maryland Registration" into Google and quickly found the registration page. Without hesitating, I grabbed my credit card and entered my information as fast as I could, clicking the registration button without a second thought. It relieved me in one sense, yet it also felt like I was carrying the weight of the world at the same time. I was about to leap, both literally and figuratively into uncharted territory.

The beauty of the unforeseen future lies in the opportunities presented. If you give yourself a chance, at the very least, you can say you tried. One of my greatest fears remains the prospect of reaching a certain stage in my life only to look back with regret, lamenting that I did not give myself a fair opportunity. I aspire to reflect on my life with pride for the decisions I made and the actions I took, knowing that I embraced the journey without hesitation.

When embarking on significant endeavors, it is all too easy to fall prey to self-doubt and question our capabilities. Thoughts may swirl in our minds, such as, "What if I train and still don't finish?" or "What if I fail?" We often allow these vulnerabilities to dominate our thought processes. A more constructive question to consider is: What if you don't try? What if you never set your sights on a monumental goal in your life? Inevitably, you will arrive at a moment in your life— whether it be at your retirement celebration or during a casual evening of bingo at a senior center—when you will reflect back with a sense of regret. You will find yourself pondering whether you truly belonged in the world of achievers. The haunting "what ifs" will linger in your mind, serving as reminders of unrealized potential.

This is a critical juncture in your journey, where the influence of your friendships and social circle becomes paramount. Surrounding yourself with a supportive network of individuals who champion your aspirations can guide you toward making progress. Conversely, if you find yourself in the company of naysayers and skeptics, you risk becoming ensnared at this crossroads, thwarted by negativity in your pursuit of growth.

Consider the hypothetical scenario in which Tom Brady chose to give up after his lackluster experience sitting on the bench for the winless Junipero Serra Junior Varsity football team. What if he had thrown in the towel after being designated as the seventh-string quarterback for the Michigan Wolverines? Or what if he had decided to retire from football after being drafted as the 199th pick in the NFL Draft, following a subpar performance at the combine?

Instead of succumbing to adversity, he leaned on his family and support network, maintaining control over the aspects of his life that he could influence. He provided comfort to his parents, Thomas Sr. and Galynn, and sought counsel and guidance from his friend Alex Guerrero. It would have been all too easy for Tom to surround himself with a less supportive group, one that might have deterred him from pursuing his dreams. Yet, through perseverance and strategic choices about the people in his life, he emerged as one of the most celebrated NFL superstars in history, now renowned for winning seven Super Bowl rings.

This aspect of preparation is essential and must be viewed as non-negotiable. To achieve success, you must surround yourself with individuals who uplift and support you rather than those who hold you back. Do not allow the weight of negativity to obstruct your path to realizing your dreams.

LIFE

During my senior year of football, we had an exceptional team, though we found ourselves ranked seventh out of just eight teams, which left us with a distinct chip on our shoulder. We began the season with remarkable momentum, winning three consecutive games and consistently proving our opponents and the league wrong.

As the season progressed, we faced an incredibly formidable opponent in Cleveland-Hill High School, a team that was bigger, stronger, and faster than us— one that we seemingly had little chance of competing against. Compounding the challenge, earlier that week, our long-time coach and friend, Mark Petersen, experienced a personal tragedy with the loss of his mother, a situation that deeply affected our entire community.

In tragic circumstances like these, people often bend or break under pressure. Despite the circumstance, Coach demonstrated incredible strength during this difficult time, and his resilience left an indelible mark on his team. As we took the field that day, we carried Coach Pete's mother in our thoughts, yet we were laser-focused on the task at hand. We stepped onto the gridiron with grit and determination, resolved to "win for Pete."

In the first quarter, we found ourselves trailing 7-0. As the clock wound down, we headed to the sideline for a pep talk, our heads hanging low. Coach Pete had a challenging task ahead of him. He spoke about life and the importance of persevering through adversity. He shared heartfelt reflections on his mother, emphasizing that just because something was once a certain way, doesn't mean it has to remain so. Looking each of us in the eyes, he urged us to focus on the present: "The future depends on each play. Don't dwell on the past. Don't worry about the future. Give your all to every single play."

We took his words to heart. The energy and focus ignited during that two-minute speech provided the motivation we desperately needed. As the game progressed, it appeared we were gaining strength while our opponents were faltering. However, this was a misperception. Our opponents were preoccupied with what had happened and what was to come, while we remained anchored in the present. Their coach had failed to inspire them.

As the final minutes of the first half ticked away, we led 21-7. Riding the momentum of the first half, we emerged after halftime ready to seize our opportunity. Although we were seen as the underdogs, we ultimately triumphed with a score of 37-13. Was it luck? Perhaps.

But this experience taught me invaluable lessons about harnessing positive energy and blocking out negativity. Motivated and influenced by Coach Pete, we refused to allow external factors to dictate our emotions. We placed our trust in him, and it paid off. Why? Because the effective use of positive influence stands as one of the greatest motivators and shapers of momentum.

IRONMAN

It was 6:35 AM on a cool, foggy morning in Maryland as I gazed out at the Choptank River. My nerves were palpable, and all I could focus on were the frigid waters, the potential of jellyfish encounters, and the memories of my earlier failure at the Olympic Triathlon. Negative thoughts swirled through my mind, leading me down a rabbit hole of fear. What if the water is too cold? What if I get stung by a jellyfish? What if I can't swim at all? What if someone pulls me under?

As I stood in silence, the weight of these thoughts grew heavier, and the unknown variables began to loom larger. We had precisely two hours and twenty minutes to complete the swim. What if I couldn't finish in time? Just a week prior, I had completed a trial swim that left me feeling confident, but that was with my mother by my side, providing the security I needed in a familiar lake. Now, in this moment of uncertainty, I scanned the crowd, hoping to see a familiar face—a glimmer of hope and support. Sadly, I was unable to locate any members of my family.

Me and Mom training on the days leading up to the Ironman. If it wasn't for my Mom, I wouldn't have been able to train properly for this event. She was more than just my watch on the lake, she is a beacon of what it means to work hard and overcome obstacles.
Barmore Photo Collection

The look of concern on my face must have conveyed my lack of self-belief to the woman standing in front of me. Her name was Mary, a long-time resident of Cambridge, Maryland, who had dedicated fifteen years of her life to volunteering at the Maryland Ironman. She had witnessed countless individuals from all walks of life and varying fitness levels take on this challenge.

As we spoke, it was clear that Mary had encountered many people with stories similar to mine. The first question she posed was, "Are you nervous?" I responded, "I think I'll be okay," to which she replied, "You are nervous, and that's a good thing because it signifies that this is important to you."

Her reassurance helped ease my anxiety. We continued to converse for several minutes, and gradually, others joined in the discussion. As I looked around, I realized I was not alone, nor were they. Mary became the beacon of hope we all needed.

All too often in life, particularly in our fitness journeys and personal growth, we find ourselves feeling as if we are drowning. It is in these moments that a connection with others can make all the difference, reminding us that we are not alone in our struggles and fears.

In the 1950s, biologist Curt Richter conducted a poignant experiment involving rats that has since become a powerful metaphor for resilience and hope. He set out to determine how long these creatures could endure in water. In his initial test, Richter placed a rat in a tank, observing as its frantic struggle to stay afloat lasted only about fifteen minutes before it began to succumb, bobbing up and down in desperation.

At this point, he intervened, rescuing the rat and allowing it to rest. In a follow-up experiment, Richter employed the same methodology, but this time, the results were astonishing. The rat persisted for an average of sixty hours. The difference? The first rat had entered the water with no expectation of rescue, while the second rat, having experienced the kindness of being saved, swam with the unwavering belief that it would be pulled from the depths if it continued to fight.

Richter's findings provide profound insight into the power of hope. When we cultivate hope and surround ourselves with a supportive community, we can overcome substantial obstacles that threaten to pull us under. In essence, the rat had developed a resilience rooted in the anticipation of rescue, reinforcing the truth that hope can be a catalyst for extraordinary endurance.

Reflecting on my own experiences, I recall the apprehension and intense nerves I felt the morning of my first ever Ironman. If it hadn't been for Mary—a compassionate stranger who offered me kindness and reassurance—I likely would have struggled to complete the swimming portion of the race. At that instant, her comforting words filled me with the courage to face my fears head-on. I could have easily surrendered to the waves of doubt and despair, plummeting to the depths of the Choptank River, overwhelmed by disbelief in my abilities. Doubt can be an imposing force, much like the cold water that threatened to engulf me. Despite the feeling of doubt and angst, Mary's unwavering belief in my potential served as a lifeline.

To this day, I wish I could reach out to her to express my gratitude for the support she provided—a beacon of hope that inspired me to embrace that challenging moment. She embodied the essence of what it means to encourage others to pursue their dreams.

As we journey through life, it is crucial to remember that we should never swim alone. Seek out those who inspire you to reach your highest potential and empower you to conquer your fears. Surround yourself with individuals who genuinely believe in your capabilities and uplift you when self-doubt threatens to drag you under. With the right support, we can cultivate resilience, fuel our hope, and achieve what once seemed impossible. The swim proved to be less of an obstacle than I had anticipated, and I owe much of that to the encouragement I received from Mary.

As I emerged from the water, I was greeted by my true support system who had been anxiously waiting for me on the shore. There stood my wife and son, my parents, my brother and sister, my brother-in-law, and my nephew and niece. Water dripped down my body, mingling with the tears streaming from my eyes as a surge of emotions overwhelmed me. In just two minutes, I laughed, smiled, and cried, all at once, but it was the unwavering presence of my family that served as the beacon of energy I desperately needed after my battle with the sea.

Throughout my life, my family has consistently been my rock, providing the foundation of support necessary to confront any challenge. My brother and sister, despite being younger than me, have always been a source of inspiration. They possess an incredible drive to not only meet expectations but to exceed them in every endeavor. I have always looked up to them, and I am confident that when they read these words, they will feel the same way. This dynamic encapsulates what I believe to be the secret to fostering personal growth within your immediate environment. When you surround yourself with individuals who are committed to inspiring one another, it creates a powerful atmosphere conducive to growth and achievement. This reciprocal motivation elevates the standard for everyone involved, encouraging all parties to push through their personal limitations.

After the Ironman, surrounded by my support squad! Nick, Julian, Jamie, Kari, Charlotte, Dad (Dean), Mom, Brian, Beckett, me, Adrienne and believe it or not, Rushy is in this picture too! He's just inside Mama's belly.
Barmore Photo Collection

In contrast, negative influences abound in life, and few need assistance in cultivating doubt or imposing boundaries on their ambitions. Therefore, it is essential to intentionally select companions who will challenge you to strive for your goals and dreams, rather than those who may inadvertently hold you back.

In my journey, I recognized that the energy generated in

such an uplifting environment can be transformative. It empowers you to confront your fears and pursue your objectives with confidence. One of the most valuable lessons I learned was that champions aren't merely those who reach the finish line first. They are often those who have a robust support system, lifting each other in times of struggle and joy alike.

As you cultivate your path toward personal development, seek out those who share your vision, who will hold you accountable, and who will celebrate your victories as if they were their own. Ultimately, the strength of a supportive network can make the difference between stagnation and growth, helping you navigate the turbulent waters of life's challenges and emerge victorious, dripping with both sea water and tears of triumph.

REFLECTION

1. Who are three people who support your big goals?

   a. _____

   b. _____

   c. _____

2. We often look for support from others. How were you willing to support somebody who supported you?

   _____

   _____

   _____

   _____

3. Are you willing to share this book with them and/or have honest conversations about growth?

   _____

   _____

   _____

   _____

CHAPTER 3

THE MIRROR

What exactly is self-assessment? To begin with, let's refer to the Merriam-Webster definition: *the act or process of analyzing and evaluating oneself or one's actions.*

Self-assessment is a crucial component of personal development, as it provides a foundation for understanding where you currently stand in various aspects of your life. When you strive for greatness—be it in personal achievements, career aspirations, or any form of self-improvement—it is essential to have a clear understanding of your starting point.

For example, if you are twenty-five-years-old and have never set foot on an ice rink, it is unlikely that setting a goal to compete in the World Figure Skating Championships is realistic or feasible. Grounding your aspirations in reality allows you to set more attainable and meaningful goals. On the other hand, it is equally important to recognize that everyone has a past, and the experiences that you have encountered along the way have shaped you into the person you are today.

Rather than allowing your previous choices or situations to define you, embrace the notion that your past has merely laid the groundwork for your current self. If you find yourself in a place that does not align with your aspirations, remember that those past decisions do not have to shackle you to the person you once were. Instead, they can serve as valuable lessons to propel you forward toward the person you wish to become. Ultimately, the responsibility for your happiness lies with you. If you are content with your current circumstances, that is an affirmation of your choices and efforts. Conversely, if you're dissatisfied with where you find yourself today, it is crucial to acknowledge that this, too, is a consequence of your own decisions.

Every day, we collectively make thousands of micro-decisions that may ripple through our lives in profound ways. Not every decision will yield a positive outcome. Some may even hinder our progress or lead us astray. The key to effective self-assessment lies in the ability to learn from your choices and mistakes without allowing them to shape your identity. Instead of becoming defined by your past or viewing them as failures, reframe those experiences as opportunities for growth. Reflect on the lessons learned and use that knowledge to identify areas for improvement in your life.

Self-assessment is not merely a process of critique. It is an opportunity for self-reflection and renewal. As you engage in self-assessment, take the time to ask yourself critical questions. What are my strengths? Where do I struggle? What actions can I take today to lead me closer to my goals? By developing a habit of regularly evaluating yourself and your choices, you will cultivate a mindset that embraces growth, accountability, and resilience. Remember, the journey to becoming your best self is ongoing and requires dedication, but it begins with the willingness to look inward and remain open to change.

LIFE

During my high school years, I excelled as a hockey goaltender and also showed promise in football, baseball, and basketball, ultimately receiving interest from colleges in three of those four sports. These athletic pursuits brought me immense joy—they came naturally to me, and my talent allowed me to thrive without much effort. I merely failed to recognize the gift that I had. I didn't fully commit to elevating my skills or taking my game to the next level.

To this day, people often ask me why I didn't pursue a higher level of competition in hockey, and while I have offered numerous justifications and excuses over the years, the truth boils down to two fundamental factors. First and foremost, the individuals in my life were not aligned with the path I aspired to take. My friends and family lacked any experience in the realm of competitive hockey. Consequently, I did not have a mentor or guiding figure to illuminate the journey I could have pursued. Instead, my social circle was focused on the familiar routine of "fun" from Thursday through Sunday. As a result, I followed suit without questioning whether this alignment truly served my aspirations. I wasn't taking control of my life nor was I accountable for my actions.

Week after week, my primary concern became the next Thirsty Thursday at the local bar, effectively marking the unofficial start of the weekend. This mentality trapped me in a cycle of mediocrity, leaving me in what felt like a twilight zone filled with unrelenting dissatisfaction and confusion regarding how to escape. At that time, I had no real sense of purpose or direction—I was simply living for the next social outing, driven by a desire to drink and spend time with my friends.

The late teens and early twenties can be a particularly disorienting period. Many individuals lack the drive to pursue the possibilities that life offers. Breaking free from a familiar cycle becomes increasingly challenging, especially when it constitutes the only reality you have ever known. This is where the opportunity for change resides. You have the power to be the catalyst that shatters an endless chain of bad luck, unproductive excuses, and pervasive regret. Embrace the ambition to establish a new chain—one that reflects growth, aspiration, and fulfillment. Be the person within your circle who shifts the narrative, transforming the status quo.

Raising the standard amongst your peers requires courage and determination, but becoming the individual who sets a higher benchmark can have a transformative impact not only on your life but on those around you. Your journey of self-improvement can inspire others to follow suit. Instead of merely floating down the river of conformity, take intentional steps toward embodying the values and goals you wish to pursue.

To create a culture of accountability and excellence, you must cultivate the mindset that refuses to accept anything less than your best. In doing so, you will not only elevate your own aspirations but may also empower those in your circle to realize their potential as well. This is the essence of true leadership— by exemplifying commitment and ambition, you can ignite a fire in others that encourages collective growth and inspires everyone involved to strive for greatness.

CHAPTER 3

IRONMAN

In 2011, my brother Brian dropped an unexpected bombshell on our family—he was going to run the Buffalo Half Marathon. My immediate reaction was one of disbelief. I thought to myself, "NO WAY!" The idea that he could take on such a monumental challenge felt impossible at the time. No one in our family had ever pursued anything even remotely close to that level of endurance. In fact, I chuckled out loud, thinking that this was an event meant for seasoned athletes, not amateurs like us. At that moment, I truly didn't grasp what a half marathon entailed, let alone the commitment required to train for one.

Unbeknownst to me at the time, Brian was laying the groundwork for what would become the foundations of the Prep-Rep-Repeat principles. Day after day, morning after morning, I witnessed my brother implement the disciplines necessary to achieve his goal. For five consecutive months, he dedicated himself to his training regimen, never straying from his path, even in the face of skepticism from those around him. He had prepared meticulously, following a well-structured plan, earning his progress through diligent repetition, and when necessary, he would return to the drawing board to reassess and refine his approach.

When race day arrived, Brian crushed his first long-distance running event, and I could see how his success illuminated a fire within me that I desperately needed at that time. Inspired by his achievement, I felt a surge of motivation. It was my turn to step up.

Three years had elapsed since Brian's announcement, and I

36

was ready to push my own boundaries further. I wanted to test my limits and see if I could achieve the same level of success. Brian devised a plan for me to follow, which I recognized as a crucial element in my preparation. Having a structured plan in place and committing to it without deviation would be essential to my success.

In 2015, I crossed the finish line of my first half marathon in under two hours—a significant accomplishment that filled me with pride. But I wasn't ready to stop there. I wanted to raise the bar even higher. Could I tackle a full marathon? The following year, during what turned out to be the hottest day of the year in Buffalo, New York, I completed my first full marathon. Each mile tested my endurance, determination, and mental fortitude, but crossing that finish line was an exhilarating triumph.

Fast forward to 2019, when the Pittsburgh Half Marathon came into view—it was another opportunity to challenge myself, and once again, I crushed it. Reflecting on these experiences, each event tested me in various ways, both mentally and physically. At the time, I failed to recognize that they were gradually preparing me for what lay ahead in 2022. Each marathon and half marathon built upon the last, forging not only my physical capabilities but also fortifying my mental resilience. These experiences underscore the importance of stepping out of your comfort zone and embracing new challenges.

Much like Brian, who initially stepped into the unknown, we all have the capacity to transcend our limitations if we are willing to commit to a plan and put in the requisite work. The journey may be fraught with obstacles, but the growth we achieve along the way is invaluable. So, whether you are contemplating your first race or simply looking to expand your horizons, remember: Each step you take—despite being daunting—brings you closer to the person you have the potential to become. Embrace the journey, believe in your capabilities, and take that leap into the unknown. You may be surprised by how far you can go.

In the spring months leading up to my Ironman in Maryland, I made an impulsive decision that would ultimately shape my journey and reinforce my commitment to personal growth. I signed up for a sprint triathlon in my hometown dubbed the "Big Fish" Triathlon. Initially, I had no intentions of participating in this event; it was merely a fleeting advertisement that caught my eye on social media. As luck would have it, it happened to be just a couple of weeks away when I decided to take the plunge and register.

I entered this new challenge with a mixture of fear, excitement, and anticipation. I had no way of knowing whether I would finish first, come in last, or even fail to finish at all. Yet, in hindsight, this decision undeniably laid the groundwork for my eventual success in the Ironman just four months later. I believed I had been training diligently and holding myself accountable until that crisp morning in Mayville, New York.

As I arrived at the event, I quickly realized I was ill-prepared for what lay ahead. I showed up without a wetsuit, without a long-sleeve jacket, and without any true understanding of the challenge I was about to face. As I scanned the crowd of approximately seventy-five participants, I soon discovered that I was one of only two individuals without a wetsuit. Anxiety began to creep in as the MC delivered a final "last call" for anyone wishing to submit a DNF (Did Not Finish).

I felt a wave of uncertainty wash over me. The only other

participant without a wetsuit laughed off the idea of entering the icy waters, declaring there was no chance she would be getting in. Was I making a monumental mistake by going through with it? Should I have followed her lead and backed out?

As I pondered these doubts and watched fellow competitors meticulously prepare their bikes and nutrition, my own feelings of inadequacy intensified. I realized I had not brought any nutritional supplements for the race, and my confidence began to wane. With every passing minute and participant that entered the water, my nervousness surged. I began inching closer to the edge of the water, and at that moment, I crossed an invisible line—you could say, a point of no return. At approximately 7:30 AM on that frigid Saturday morning, I took my first step into Chautauqua Lake, where the temperature hovered around 59 degrees.

I had been reassured by several seasoned racers that the water would feel warmer than the air, but I quickly discovered that they were unequivocally mistaken. They were wrong in a way that I would soon learn the true meaning of being thrown into the deep end—quite literally. Before that day, my training had primarily consisted of swimming in the comfortable confines of a local pool for about a month. Nothing could have prepared me for this shocking transition from the serene environment of the swimming pool to the murky, cold waters of the lake.

As the reality of my situation set in, I recognized that preparing for any challenge—whether it's a triathlon or another significant life goal—requires not just commitment but also a thorough understanding of what lies ahead. This experience sparked a fire within me that would carry me through my training and beyond. Sometimes, the path to growth is riddled with doubts and challenges. It's precisely in moments of uncertainty that we discover our true strength.

As I navigated that experience, I learned valuable lessons about resilience, adaptability, and the importance of preparation. In life, the decisions we make—including those made in haste—can lead us to profound revelations and growth opportunities. Embrace the challenges before you, for every moment of discomfort could be a catalyst for change and self-discovery. Each race, each hurdle, and each experience is a step towards becoming the person we aspire to be.

I didn't fully grasp the formidable power of natural water until I found myself approximately fifty yards into the race. That's when reality hit me—I was in for a challenging day. Almost immediately, I was caught off guard by a wave that felt as though it towered ten feet high. In truth, it was likely the splash from a puddle, but right then, it seemed monumental. The force knocked my goggles askew, sending them off-center on my face. Instinctively, I reached up to adjust them, but my efforts only made the situation worse. Frustrated, I made the rash decision to tear them off entirely and place them on the top of my head. I swam awkwardly for about thirty feet with the goggles perched above my brow, doing my best to keep pace with the other competitors. Eventually, they slipped completely off and sank to the lake's bottom.

Losing those goggles felt akin to dropping the Heart of the Ocean diamond from the movie *Titanic*. The loss was devastating. They symbolized my connection to the race and my confidence in completing it. But at that moment, I realized I had to let them go and redirect my focus to the water and each stroke ahead. Doubt began to creep in as my mind raced with uncertainty. I teetered on the edge of a mental crossroads— should I give up or forge ahead?

As the rest of the participants began to pull away from me, I found myself questioning whether I would even survive the swim, let alone finish the race. With every stroke, I fought not just against the water but for my own sense of purpose. The water felt like a dark abyss, threatening to swallow me whole, never to be recovered. Despite my fears, I continually reminded myself to focus on just one more stroke, rather than contemplating how to escape the water or thinking about the finish line. I reminded myself that I didn't need to be Michael Phelps. I didn't have to catch up to the rest of the pack. I only needed to concentrate on making one stroke, then another, and then another. It had to get easier, didn't it? WRONG!

At that point, my visibility had plummeted to near zero, my goggles surrendered to the depths of Chautauqua Lake. With each wave crashing over me, I felt the water seep into my eyes, blurring my vision further. The chill of the water intensified, sending shivers down my spine, and I felt the hairs on the back of my neck stand on end.

The combined fear of the unknown ahead and the relentless cold presented challenges I hadn't anticipated. As I swam, my toes grew numb, and the sensation in my fingers began to fade. Hope started to slip away as quickly as my feeling did. But on that unique circumstance of despair, I knew I needed to shift my focus. I consciously turned my internal dialogue from negative to positive, reminding myself, ONE MORE! I repeated it like a mantra. If I could get through one more stroke, it would naturally lead to another and another after that.

I understood that on that Saturday morning, I wouldn't be breaking any world records, but that wasn't the point. This experience embodies a crucial lesson in resilience: life often throws unexpected challenges our way, and it is our response to those challenges that defines us. In moments of difficulty, we must concentrate on incremental progress rather than fixating on the larger goal. Each small step we take, no matter how daunting the journey might seem, is a testament to our willpower and determination. Embrace those moments of fear and uncertainty. They are the true proving grounds for our strength. Rather than succumb to the overwhelming weight of the struggle, we must commit to taking that next stroke, letting go of what weighs us down, and staying focused on inching our way forward. After all, those tiny victories add up, and they pave the way for monumental achievements.

My singular goal at that moment was simply to make it to shore. It's remarkable how time can feel as though it stands still when you are in the throes of agony. What felt like an endless five miles was, in reality, only a quarter of the distance. As I rounded the first buoy, the weight of knowing I still had three-quarters of the swim left to conquer drained my already diminishing hope. Nonetheless, I found there was still one more paddle left in me.

In an effort to regain some control over my predicament, I transitioned from the breaststroke to the freestyle, then back to the backstroke. To occupy my mind and distract myself from the sheer misery of the experience, I began a mental counting exercise. I was determined to count seventy strokes in freestyle, seventy in breaststroke, and then seventy on my back.

Over and over, I repeated this routine, attempting to block out the discomfort and fatigue that threatened to consume me. Quitting was no longer an option. I had come too far to entertain such thoughts. At that point, I felt as though I was finally settling into a rhythm when, out of the corner of my eye, I caught sight of a kayak inching closer to me. "Seventy breaststroke...." I was so engrossed in each stroke that I hadn't registered how close I was to the exit ramp. "Seventy backstroke...."

And just like that, it happened—I had done it. The sensation was akin to having crossed the English Channel, yet regardless of the hyperbole, I finally exited the water.

To this day, I feel fortunate to have survived that swim. As I reached the shoreline, my legs felt like jelly, my spirit was battered, and I noticed that the participant ahead of me was already a couple of miles into his bike ride. My family and fellow supporters cheered me on encouragingly, but I struggled to pull myself together. One more step, I thought to myself—just give me one more. Despite what I deeply desired, my legs were not functioning as they should have been. I had just subjected them to an extreme session of cold water therapy, and it felt like millions of needles were pricking at my legs, extending all the way down to my toes.

Gradually, I made my way to my bike. As I arrived, I quickly consumed the only granola bar I had packed and chugged down a Gatorade in a desperate attempt to fuel my body. The cramping I experienced was unlike anything I had ever encountered before. I had heard the term "bonking" used in reference to athletes hitting a wall, but until that moment, I had never truly understood its meaning. It would have been easy to fall into a pit of despair, but I knew that now was not the time for self-pity. Instead, it was time to double down on my commitment and find a way to get on my bike, doing the exact opposite of what my mind was telling me—"You can't do this."

Amidst the chaos of thoughts swirling in my mind and the

physical discomfort wreaking havoc on my body, I recognized that this moment was a true test of my resolve. Every challenge we face presents an opportunity for growth, as it forces us to confront our limitations and push beyond them. I reminded myself that adversity breeds resilience, and triumph comes from persevering in the face of hardship. The journey may be fraught with obstacles, but it is how we navigate those challenges that determines not only our success at that juncture but also shapes the person we become in the process.

Following the swim at the Big Fish Triathlon, not knowing if I'd be able to get on the bike and continue on. This was easily the hardest challenge, mentally and physically I've ever done to this day. The orange Gatorade for the win!
Barmore Photo Collection

As I prepared to mount my bike, I understood that this race was not just about the end result; it was about the journey—the struggles, the determination, and the relentless spirit to keep moving forward. Each stroke, each moment of discomfort, and each ounce of perseverance would ultimately carve out a path to achievement. I was ready to embrace the next leg of the race, armed with the knowledge that I could overcome whatever lay ahead. So, as I clipped into my bike and took off down the course, I kept the mantra in my mind: One more step, one more pedal stroke, one more moment of courage. That was what enduring growth was made of.

Part two of the race was officially underway—the bike leg! As I pedaled away, an unsettling realization began to wash over me. My body was literally shutting down. Each stroke of the pedals intensified my awareness of the lactic acid building up, causing discomfort that radiated from my nose to my toes. I could feel my body revolting against me as I attempted to increase my speed.

The distance between me and the cyclist in front seemed insurmountable and I felt an overwhelming urge to push beyond every mental and physical limit in an effort to catch up. There was absolutely no way I was going to finish this event in last place. That was simply not an option I could accept. In the face of fatigue and the desire to surrender, I was tempted to wave the white flag of defeat. Yet, I consciously refused to grant myself that option. After expending so much mental and physical energy in the water, I began to question how I would cope with the demanding bike segment. But then it hit me— what worked for me in the swim? How did I conquer that physical distress?

Many days of training on the road paid off.
Barmore Photo Collection

The answer was simple: Counting. Yes, counting! It was a technique I had relied upon in the water to distract myself from pain and fatigue, and I recognized that I could employ it again during this ride. As I focused on the road ahead, I began to pass one cyclist, then another, and another. Each rotation of the pedals was accompanied by a mantra I repeated in my head: "Up, down, and all around." I concentrated on each pedal stroke, counting each rotation and immersing myself in the motion. I echoed the strategies I used in the water—seventy hard pedals followed by seventy easy ones.

This mental exercise allowed me to divert my focus from the physical strain to a manageable task—seventy repetitions to jog my mind and shift my concentration. Gradually, I found myself smiling as I looked around. By shifting my attention away from the discomfort in my body and toward the surroundings, I created a space of positivity amid the struggle.

To my amazement, I ended up passing ten athletes along the way. I was pushing the limits of my endurance, refusing to accept anything less than my very best at that moment. It is in these challenging times that we truly discover the depths of our mental toughness. We often train and prepare our bodies for the physical challenges ahead, yet it is in the extremes that the real battle lies in our minds. Our mental dialogue has a powerful influence on our actions, often whispering discouragement with phrases like, "I'm dying," or "I can't go on."

In those moments, it is essential to recognize that these thoughts reside in our minds and do not reflect our actual capabilities. To triumph, we must cultivate an uncommon will to silence that internal voice and press forward, taking one stroke and one pedal at a time. As I cruised into the transition area from my bike, I felt as if I had just conquered the world with what I had accomplished. The sense of triumph was fleeting, as I was quickly reminded that I was still nowhere near the finish line.

I had invested everything into my cycling efforts in a

desperate attempt to catch up, and in doing so, I gained a firsthand understanding of what it truly meant to feel depleted. This marked the second time that day I had encountered that intense sensation of exhaustion. Dismounting from my bike, I thought I might not have the capacity to push any further. Yet, even in that overwhelming fatigue, I realized I hadn't journeyed this far just to stop now. It became clear to me that progress isn't merely about crossing the finish line—it's about the determination to keep moving forward, regardless of the obstacles we face. Each challenge faced is an opportunity to strengthen our resolve, and each stroke we take is a testament to our tenacity. So, I steadied myself, took a deep breath, and prepared to take the next step on this tumultuous yet rewarding journey.

As soon as my feet hit the ground, they betrayed me completely, and I collapsed. My legs could no longer support my body weight, and I first fell to my knees before using my bike as a crutch to hoist myself up. Slowly and unsteadily, I hobbled into the transition area, gathering myself as best I could in order to get back on my feet. I was now two-thirds of the way done with the race, an incredible feat in itself. Yet, as I cast my eyes toward the finish line, I realized, much to my dismay, that I was still heading in the opposite direction.

At that moment, my body and my mind were utterly exhausted. The run was a mere six miles long—something I had completed countless times in training leading up to this weekend. I kept hoping that at some point, my natural athletic ability would kick in, and the lingering effects of my earlier meltdown or "bonking" would fade away. I was mistaken!

I quickly learned that I had little to no experience with triathlons, and because of this lack of familiarity, I had failed to plan adequately for the challenge before me. When you're embarking on something you've never done before, having a solid plan is essential—one that you must trust and commit to. If it requires you to invest in guidance or resources, then absolutely do so. Don't make the same mistakes I did by approaching a challenge without a well-defined blueprint.

As I began running, it felt as if I was dragging a piano while wearing lead-filled shoes, each step a monumental effort. I reached the half-mile mark and paused to contemplate whether I could go any further. It was then that the other participants I had worked so hard to pass started to reappear, as they continued with their strong strides. But just as my doubts began to consume me, I looked up and spotted my family—my wife, my son, my parents, and my brother—waiting for me with open arms. Tears filled my eyes, but this time they were tears of joy, transcending the pain and exhaustion I had endured. In that very moment, as the emotional weight of our connection washed over me, I felt a surge of courage fill my heart. I realized that they were my goal. They were the reason I needed to push beyond the physical and mental fatigue.

My singular focus shifted from the race itself to reaching my family. I wasn't thinking about the next mile or the finish line. I just needed to reach them. I took a brief moment to gather my emotions, say hello, and reassure them that I was alright. I gulped down a cup of ice-cold water, exchanged high fives, shared smiles and laughter, and then I hit the road again. Yet, as I distanced myself from my support system, I felt a wave of loneliness wash over me once more.

It was crucial that I regain my focus and mentality. I turned back to the road, and strangely enough, as I created distance between myself and my family, my energy levels began to rise.

Little by little, I kept moving forward. I recalled Martin Luther King, Jr.'s powerful words, "If you can't fly, run. If you can't run, walk. If you can't walk, crawl, but whatever you do, you have to keep moving forward."

This was at the turn when I didn't want to leave my family. I had misty eyes and didn't know if I could finish but I kept them in mind for the remainder of that event. Make sure your environment is right if you're chasing grander destinations.
Barmore Photo Collection

I held tightly to this mantra, allowing it to accompany me every agonizing step of the next two and a half miles. I never resorted to crawling, even though there were moments when it felt like my only option. Each step was a stark reminder of the importance of preparation in achieving anything great. My feet pounded against the hot pavement, one step after another. By that point, the sun had emerged, intensifying the heat. I unzipped my suit, trying to allow my skin to breathe and my lungs to expand as I continued running.

I kept my gaze downward while lifting my chin, determined to maintain my focus. While I sensed that I had passed a few runners, I quickly realized I wasn't competing against anyone but myself. The winding road ahead appeared never-ending, a grueling stretch in the middle of the six-mile run that began to test my resolve. With every corner I turned, I hoped it would finally lead me to the turnaround point. Time and again, I faced disappointment as I pushed onward. Finally, I reached the halfway point, where my family awaited me once more, cheering me on with unwavering support. The sight of them reignited the energy within me, bolstering my spirit for the second half of the run.

As I turned to continue on, I called back to them, half-jokingly declaring, "All I want is a ham sandwich, a Gatorade, and to be finished!"

My Dad's voice rang out, "You'd better finish!"

As I continued to run, my pace gradually quickened, driven by the vivid image in my mind of holding my wife and my son closely, alongside the tantalizing thought of a warm ham sandwich. The overwhelming desire to distance myself from the grueling course urged me forward. All I wanted was to complete this challenge and never have to think about it again.

As I powered through miles four and five, I felt a transformation taking place—I was moving like wildfire, charged with a newfound momentum that felt almost exhilarating. In that moment, I recalled an essential truth: repetition eliminates fear. Practice builds courage and cultivates strength. With each stride, I began to reclaim my confidence, reminding myself that I was capable. I was starting to believe in my abilities again!

As I turned the final corner, a surge of adrenaline coursed through my veins. I felt invincible, reminiscent of Usain Bolt sprinting toward victory at the 2016 Olympics in Rio de Janeiro. My heart raced not only from the exertion but also from the intoxicating sight of my family cheering me on and the finish line coming into view. I could practically smell the ham sandwich and taste the Gatorade, sensations that promised relief and rejuvenation after the taxing journey I had just endured.

Fueled by the encouragement of my loved ones and the vision of my goal, I shifted into what felt like another gear, sprinting toward the checkered flag with all the determination and ferocity I could muster. And then it happened. I crossed the finish line.

Right then, the thrill of completion washed over me, although I would be remiss not to acknowledge that it felt somewhat anticlimactic, a "stale" victory if you will. Nonetheless, despite that initial feeling, it was undeniably a personal victory. I had done it. I was now a triathlon finisher.

Each race represents more than just a completion. It stands as a testament to resilience, determination, and the willingness to confront the trials that life throws our way. Achieving this milestone wasn't merely about crossing the finish line. It symbolized the culmination of hard work, the overcoming of mental barriers, and the relentless pursuit of a goal. In that brief time of triumph, I realized that the true essence of any challenge lies not in the accolades we receive, but in the growth we experience along the journey.

This lesson, though rooted in my triathlon experience, extends far beyond athleticism. It underscores the importance of perseverance, the power of positive imagery, and the potential that resides within each of us to push through adversity. When faced with moments of doubt or fatigue, remember, you have the strength to keep moving forward. The victory may lie in the journey, and with each step, you reinforce the idea that you are capable of achieving greatness, one small repetition at a time. So, embrace each challenge, believe in yourself, and sprint toward your own metaphorical finish line.

Of all the long-distance events I have participated in, including my formidable Ironman, this particular event stands out as my greatest physical and mental accomplishment, and I suspect it will always hold that distinction. From the moment I stepped into the water to the instant I crossed the finish line, I consciously set aside all doubts and fears, anchoring my focus on just one more stroke, followed by one more pedal, and then one more step. This mindset not only allowed me to complete the triathlon, but also instilled in me the resilience and mental fortitude necessary for my Ironman journey and, indeed, for all facets of my life.

In this race, I learned the power of perseverance. Each stroke and every pedal revolved around that single philosophy of focusing on what I could control, rather than being overwhelmed by the challenge ahead. It transformed my experience from one overshadowed by anxiety to one characterized by determination and grit. When I finally pushed through to the finish line, I felt a profound sense of accomplishment wash over me. I may have left before the awards were presented, but the reality is that I achieved 3rd place in my age bracket.

Admittedly, I'm pretty certain that there were only three participants in that category, but this acknowledgment did little to diminish my pride. The coffee mug I received for my accomplishment at the Big Fish Triathlon will always be cherished far more than any shiny medal I've ever earned. Its significance transcends the ordinary recognition of achievement. It symbolizes hope, perseverance, and the belief that I could overcome challenges. To me, that mug isn't merely a trophy to display. It is a constant reminder that through hard work and dedication, I can accomplish anything I set my mind to, regardless of the obstacles in my path.

And let me not forget to mention the ham sandwich waiting for me. It was everything I had hoped for—warm, satisfying, and a perfect reward after a grueling experience. Beyond its savory goodness, it signified the completion of my journey that day. My victory, my accomplishment, and the sheer joy of having achieved something that once felt insurmountable. Every step of that journey—from the initial moments of doubt to crossing the finish line—taught me invaluable lessons about perseverance, mental strength, and the importance of celebrating even the smallest victories.

Whether you're engaged in a fierce competition or navigating the challenges of everyday life, remember that each small action you take contributes to the greater story of your success. Embrace your journey, focus on the next step, and hold tightly to the belief that you can achieve greatness. Let that belief act as your guiding light, propelling you forward with courage, determination, and the hopeful anticipation of what lies ahead.

REFLECTION

1. What are the three things that you value the most?

    a. _____

    b. _____

    c. _____

2. What is something you once couldn't do but now you can?

    _____

    _____

    _____

    _____

3. What is one thing on your "bucket list"? Something that you plan on doing in the future?

    _____

    _____

    _____

    _____

CHAPTER 4

MILE MARKERS & MILESTONES

When setting a goal for yourself, it's essential to make that goal as grand and ambitious as you can mentally and physically envision. When you establish a larger-than-life expectation, it not only motivates you but also helps you achieve several smaller objectives along the way, thereby fostering a sense of self-instilled confidence. As you prepare to pursue this big-picture goal, you will encounter various "mile markers"—evidence along your journey that demonstrates that success is not only possible but fully within your reach.

Kobe Bryant once famously said, "I'm chasing perfection even though I know I will never catch it. Just the fact that I was willing to chase it means I can defeat most of my opponents because most of my opponents will never chase something."

These words resonate with me deeply, serving as guiding principles for my own endeavors. The milestones you achieve along the way—these mile markers—are micro-wins that bolster your courage and propel you toward your ultimate objectives. Over time, these small victories can accumulate to create significant momentum, moving you closer to your destination.

With all of that, it's crucial to recognize that these milestone victories are not always glamorous. They often lack the fanfare that larger accomplishments receive and may go unnoticed. For instance, one daily micro-win that I strive to achieve is drinking a gallon of water. This seemingly simple act promotes a healthy lifestyle, and it has significantly contributed to my training for an Ironman. While I may take this habit for granted now, it took considerable time and effort to build it into my routine.

We must not undervalue these mile marker victories as they are vital stepping stones in the process of living an "Iron Life." They lead you toward larger milestones that are often celebrated more widely. For example, if you are training to complete a distance of ten miles within a certain time frame and you accomplish that goal, that is a milestone worth recognizing. When you achieve these temporary milestones, it feels akin to reaching the light at the end of a tunnel. You may actually be surprised to find that this is not merely an endpoint. Instead, it marks the beginning of a new journey into the next phase of your expedition.

Life is a continuous cycle of setting ambitious goals, achieving micro-wins, and celebrating milestones. With each step forward, you build resilience, foster confidence, and develop the grit necessary to tackle the challenges that lie ahead. As you embark on your journey toward your grand ambitions, remember to celebrate each mile marker along the way. Each small victory not only contributes to your growth but also prepares you for the next tunnel you must navigate. Embrace the process, find joy in the journey, and let every victory—big or small—ignite the flame of determination within you, guiding you further along your path to success.

LIFE

Until I was thirty-two-years-old, I held a vague and unclear understanding of where I wanted to go and what I wanted to accomplish in life. In hindsight, I don't just think of it as a blurred vision. I recognize that I was essentially blind to my true aspirations. Despite countless college courses that laid out frameworks for setting goals and following through, I never managed to connect the dots. I failed to apply the principles I had learned to my life, and as a direct result, it took me an arduous amount of time to discover meaning and purpose.

Life tends to become stagnant when you overlook the significance of milestone markers, celebrate your achievements, and genuinely comprehend the importance of progress. If you journey through life without acknowledging these key elements, you may find true happiness elusive. One fundamental principle that can alter your life's trajectory is the act of writing down your goals on a sheet of paper. Yes, it truly is as simple as that!

Grab a pen, find a piece of paper, and start writing. Unfortunately, many people hear this suggestion and dismiss its relevance. Yet I can attest to the transformative power of physically writing down your intentions and aspirations. Underneath your main goal, list three to five actionable steps that will help you attain that ultimate dream. The first time I employed this approach, I wrote down my desire to lose thirty pounds.

At that time, I was not only overweight but also overindulging in alcohol, contributing to a toxic environment for myself. My evenings often consisted of ordering takeout several times a week, and I was heading down a dead-end road. While I don't consider myself a guru, and I certainly lack the ability to wave a magical wand to unlock the secrets to living an 'Iron Life,' I can share a proven method that has worked not only for me but for countless others.

A pivotal moment in my journey came in the form of a quantum leap: the simple act of putting ink to paper. By writing down my goals and placing that paper in a visible location, I forced myself to confront my aspirations daily. I made it a point to hang my goal sheet in a spot where I would see it every single day. For me, that critical location was beside my bathroom mirror. Every morning before work and every night before bed, I was greeted by the tangible reminder of my ambitions. There were indeed days when I woke up, trudged toward the bathroom, and felt an internal resistance to fully committing to my goals. The sight of my script hanging on the wall served as a constant reminder that I had goals to pursue and a person I wanted to become. It provided just enough motivation to push me toward my training regimen.

So, I encourage you, take that essential first step. Put ink on paper, and then follow up with action. Your goals deserve to be recognized, not just thought about but embraced wholeheartedly. Here's what my goal sheet looked like when I initially created it. Each word was a stepping stone guiding me toward change and progress—a blueprint for the inspiring life I envisioned. Remember, the journey toward self-improvement begins with clarity, commitment, and the courage to take that first step. Don't underestimate the power of putting pen to paper. It may very well be the catalyst for the incredible transformation you seek. This is what my goal sheet looked like.

Lose 30 Pounds
- **Be able to do seventy pushups without breaking within three weeks.**
- **Run a 5k in 24:00 or better by the time the eight weeks is up.**
- **Lose ten pounds every two weeks.**

This isn't rocket science, it's an effective accountability tactic that you can easily adopt. To achieve your goals, you must be crystal clear about what you want to accomplish, as well as, how you intend to go about it. Specificity is key!

When you clearly define your objectives, it enables you to track your progress and identify any setbacks with precision. Having concrete goals allows you to evaluate your journey, making the path to achievement much more manageable. Another crucial element you should incorporate into your goal-setting process is establishing a clear timeframe for reaching each milestone. Rather than aimlessly jotting down your aspirations and chasing thin air like a headless chicken, be precise and concrete with your intentions—and set deadlines that are etched in stone. Do not allow for any negotiation regarding these timelines.

Without a timeline, you run the risk of failing to hold yourself accountable because there will be no urgency anchoring your progress. You lack a frame of reference in terms of time. Each day can easily transform into another opportunity to procrastinate. You might find yourself saying, "I can wait until tomorrow," and before you know it, this rationale becomes your new normal.

Without that structured timeline, procrastination can easily take root and grow. For instance, I was able to lose thirty pounds within an eight week timeframe by diligently following through with my plan. It wasn't a stroll in the park. There were moments when the voice of internal negativity loomed large, trying to negotiate my commitment to the process. I learned through trial and tribulation to combat those thoughts by focusing on the significance of my goals.

Your objectives must hold weight and they should resonate

deeply with you and be of paramount importance. They should eclipse any excuses you might conjure. Ask yourself: Does your goal outweigh your justifications for why you can't achieve it?

Make certain that your ultimate goal is something that you value more than the fleeting comforts of complacency. When your goal is more important than your excuses, you empower yourself to overcome obstacles, silence doubts, and foster faith in your own abilities. In summary, accountability begins with clarity. Establish clear, specific goals and surround them with firm timelines that force you to act. When you lay out your ambitions with laser-like focus and infuse them with a sense of urgency, you'll foster a mindset dedicated to relentlessly pursuing your vision of success. By doing so, you engage a transformative process that ignites your motivation and propels you forward—one purposeful step at a time. Embrace this strategy, and watch as you turn your aspirations into accomplishments.

Ironman

The goal was set in stone: Ironman. Cambridge, Maryland. September 17, 2022. The reason I had picked Cambridge was because my inspiration at the time, Jamie, had just done it and although she expressed the angst of the jellyfish, she said it was a flat course. I was sold. This was the grand vision I had etched into my mind—the ultimate challenge that lay ahead of me. There was no turning back. The commitment was made, and it felt both exhilarating and daunting. Although I had no prior experience in Ironman Triathlons and very little knowledge about what I was getting myself into, I had one critical element in my favor: a well-defined goal.

In the preliminary stages, I had loosely developed a fitness routine based on what had once helped me prepare for long-distance events. I naively believed that by strengthening my running, the swimming and biking components would naturally fall into place with relative ease. That belief, however, was quickly shattered at the Big Fish Triathlon, where I faced unforeseen challenges that left me questioning my approach and commitment.

After the event, I turned to my wife, Adrienne, and expressed the urgency of going "all-in" if I wanted to be adequately prepared for the Ironman. I understood that half-hearted measures would not suffice. I needed a comprehensive training plan tailored to my unique needs. Looking me squarely in the eye, Adrienne asked, "What took you so long?"

Her unwavering support and candidness struck me deeply. That's the kind of partner she is—my number one supporter, always pushing me to rise to my fullest potential.

Determined to take this challenge seriously, I set out that same day to find professional coaching. I needed guidance that would ensure I was meticulously prepared for my big event. As a child, I had spent countless hours in a pool, splashing around, and biking down the dirt track behind my childhood home. I believed the old saying, "It's just like riding a bike," would hold true, allowing me to pick up where I had left off. I came to realize that I had severely underestimated the demands of both swimming and cycling over long distances. Riding my bike to the corner store was a far cry from tackling a grueling 112-mile course, and yet, that's exactly what I attempted to do.

My initial misconception about focusing solely on my running was a significant miscalculation. I quickly learned the importance of dedicating equal attention to all three elements of the triathlon. It was time for me to level up, not only in terms of physical training but also in the mental and tactical preparation required for this monumental challenge. To solidify my commitment, I made a decision that would dramatically shift my daily routine.

Every morning, my alarm clock would jolt me awake at 3:37 AM. By 3:40 AM, I was already on my feet, fueling my body for the day ahead and preparing my mind for the rigorous training sessions that awaited me. On Mondays, Wednesdays, and Fridays, I focused on running and biking, setting a disciplined schedule that would bolster my endurance and technique in both disciplines.

Each early morning workout became more than just training sessions. They represented a commitment to my growth and a testament to my resolve. With every drop of sweat and every pedal stroke, I drew closer to my goal, fortified by the understanding that success relies not just on physical ability, but also on unwavering dedication and preparation. The path to achieving lofty goals may be riddled with challenges and setbacks, but it is our response to those hurdles that ultimately shapes our journey. Embrace the process, trust the plan you create, and ensure that every action you take aligns with your vision for success. As you move forward, remember that every little effort builds upon itself. Each step, each stroke, and each pedal takes you closer to the finish line—where your dreams await.

Most runs took place on the treadmill in the early months of my training. Living in an area where safe outdoor running paths were limited until around April, I found myself confined to the gym. Outdoor running and biking were simply not feasible during the winter months, but I capitalized on the time I had. On Tuesdays and Thursdays, I would supplement my training with additional miles on the treadmill, followed by swimming sessions at the local pool.

Saturdays became my long training days, where I committed to extensive indoor spin bike sessions or ventured out for long bike rides, invariably followed by a run. Some Saturdays, I would find myself on the road for up to seven hours. It was a considerable challenge for my body, but even more taxing was the toll it took on my mind. Each Saturday morning, I would leave Adrienne and our son, Beckett, behind, and though I thought about them frequently while I was grinding through my sessions, we both understood the critical importance of those long distances in my preparation for the Ironman.

On Sundays, I would make every effort to get into the pool or venture into open water. As the weather started to improve, I finally had the opportunity to swim in Chautauqua Lake, gradually building my confidence to confront tougher elements. There were several swims when the water was tumultuous, with white caps crashing against one another.

One particular training session stands out in my mind. It was a particularly windy day, and my Dad implored me not to enter the water. Despite his concerns, my brother came alongside me in a kayak, supporting me as I faced the rough conditions. I remember swimming approximately 100 yards before stopping to grab the nose of his kayak, feeling scared and overwhelmed by the intense water and blustery winds. That experience served as a pivotal moment, and I resolved that it would be the last time I entered the water under unsafe conditions.

Each day of training tested me both physically and mentally, yet with every session, I sharpened the tools I would need to perform optimally in Maryland. It's important to preface what follows by acknowledging that I am just an average guy striving to live an "Iron Life" at this stage. What you will see below may seem quite "vanilla," a basic outline compared to elaborate plans others might employ. I've come to realize that sometimes the most straightforward strategies yield the most significant accolades in both life and fitness.

With that in mind, here is my monthly breakdown of my goal sheet leading up to September. This outline reflects the dedication and commitment I put into my training, serving as a reminder that no matter how ordinary it may appear, consistent effort and straightforward goals can lead to extraordinary outcomes. Remember, every journey begins with actionable steps, and it's these seemingly small milestones that lay the groundwork for monumental achievements. In sharing my experience, I hope to inspire you to embrace your own path toward growth, recognizing that the fundamentals can pave the way to greatness.

<u>JUNE</u>

Swim 1 Mile without using the breast stroke by the end of June.

Run a 10k in under an hour by the end of June.

Bike around Chautauqua Lake in under 3 hours by the end of June.

<u>JULY</u>

Complete a Sprint Triathlon by the end of Summer with confidence.

Bike 35 Miles in 2 hours or less by the end of July.

Swim 1 Mile in less than an hour by the end of July.

AUGUST

Swim 2.4 Miles in under 2 hours and 20 minutes by the
end of August.

Bike 100 Miles in under 6 hours by the end of August.

Run 20 Miles in less than 3 hours by the end of August.

As you can see from this example, each milestone is meticulously broken down, featuring specific times, distances, and deadlines. This clarity allowed me to understand exactly what I needed to accomplish and when, establishing a structured timeline leading to success. The path to developing personal goals and executing plans at an optimal level is not shrouded in secrecy, however, we often complicate matters unnecessarily.

In our digital age, we are inundated with an overwhelming amount of information available online. This over saturation can cloud our judgment and lead us to overanalyze our decisions. This tendency to overthink is a common pitfall known as "paralysis by analysis." We become so consumed by the details that we fail to act, ultimately preventing ourselves from moving forward. It's essential to break free from this cycle. Instead of getting lost in the minutiae, it's time to simplify your approach. Keep it straightforward, but ensure that your goals remain clear and concise.

Begin by taking stock of your journey—reflect on where you started, evaluate where you currently stand, and define where you wish to go. These elements provide a roadmap, guiding your steps and illuminating your path forward. Writing your goals down on paper is a powerful step in this process. Once you have them articulated, find a prominent place to display them—somewhere you'll see them each and every day. This constant visibility serves as a daily reminder of your ambitions, helping to keep you focused and motivated.

Consistency is vital. Following through with your goals requires daily commitment, and every small step you take brings you closer to your desired destination. By simplifying the process, maintaining awareness of your journey, and holding yourself accountable, you can overcome the inertia that often accompanies goal-setting. Remember, the journey to success doesn't have to be extravagant or complicated. It is built on the foundation of clear intentions and consistent actions. Allow yourself to embrace the simplicity of the path ahead and trust in your ability to achieve what you set out to do. You possess the power to transform your dreams into tangible results—just take that first step and keep moving forward.

Part 2
REP

CHAPTER 5

IGNITE THE ROCKET

No matter the area of life you are looking to improve, launching into a new challenge often comes with a rush of natural momentum. This initial energy is reminiscent of the excitement you feel when you sit down to write your New Year's resolutions or the enthusiasm that surges as you embark on a new DIY project. It's a universal truth. We tend to experience a surge of acute enthusiasm when starting something new. With visions of grandeur, we are filled with hopes of what we can achieve, and often the people around us amplify that energy, offering words of encouragement like, "You've got this!" or "You're going to crush it this time!"

What commonly occurs, particularly on that first Monday of the new venture is not what we expected. We dive in with all we've got, only to find ourselves just as quickly retreating back into our old habits. Driven by adrenaline, we might hit the ground running with a commitment level of 120%, eager to make changes at the snap of our fingers. But after completing that first workout, we rush to the scale, anxiously checking the mirror for any signs of transformation. More often than not, we're met with minimal progress, if any at all, leaving us with a sinking feeling of defeat.

This initial burst of enthusiasm, while invigorating, is fleeting. It's essential to recognize that this natural momentum can only carry us so far. Much like the tale of the boy who cried wolf, relying solely on that initial excitement is inherently unreliable. It cannot be counted on to sustain the journey ahead.

As the realities of commitment set in, the path to lasting change can feel daunting. Challenges arise, old habits attempt to creep back in, and that early enthusiasm begins to wane. This realization is crucial, as it prompts us to dig deeper and cultivate a sense of resilience that goes beyond surface-level motivation. While it is natural to experience that initial spark of excitement, true growth requires establishing consistent habits and a steadfast commitment to your goals.

Rather than depending solely on fleeting moments of enthusiasm, we must develop an unwavering resolve that will carry us through the inevitable trials we will face on our journeys. Think of your goals as a marathon rather than a sprint. It requires endurance, patience, and a willingness to adapt. By setting realistic expectations, creating a structured plan, and maintaining a focus on small, incremental progress—your metaphorical "mile markers" along the way—you'll develop a steadiness that will serve you far better than a sporadic fire of enthusiasm.

Embrace the fact that change is a process, not an event. Prepare to put in the effort required to sustain your momentum long after the initial excitement has faded. Stay committed to that inner voice that whispers encouragement, reminding you that even when the going gets tough, you have the strength to move forward. With time and dedication, you can transform that initial burst of inspiration into lasting achievement, paving the way for continual growth and success in every aspect of your life.

So, what do we do when we find that initial momentum waning? We must become architects of our own momentum. It sounds deceptively simple, doesn't it? But how do we actually create it? Is there a magical formula or a secret incantation that we can invoke?

When doubt creeps in and hesitation takes hold, it's crucial that we unleash the fire within us to combat that inner voice urging us to take a day off or to give ourselves an escape. Too often, we engage in internal dialogues that permit us to take a step back, allowing our self-discipline to bend. While bending once may not seem like a significant issue, repeatedly yielding to that voice will gradually erode our inner strength, leading to a breakdown in discipline.

As many of us have learned, a lack of discipline opens the door to failure, resulting in yet another broken dream. In those moments of uncertainty, it is imperative that we push ourselves to take decisive action—even when every fiber of our being tells us to remain inactive. There will be days, perhaps long stretches of time, when it feels overwhelmingly difficult to muster the energy or motivation to get on your feet.

These are the moments of truth, the pivotal juncture where you must choose your path. Will you allow yourself to be let off the hook, or will you become your own catalyst for change? In these moments of apprehension, it's all too easy to fabricate excuses and conjure up falsehoods that forfeit your ambition, leading you toward the nearest exit. It doesn't matter how challenging the task may seem, how cold the weather is, or even that your favorite green shirt is in the wash. Those are merely distractions. The only thing that matters is finding the courage to put one foot in front of the other and take those initial steps.

71

Step one is simply taking that first step.

While it may be the most daunting element of your journey—often because it necessitates confronting the fear of the unknown, understanding that this is a normal part of growth can empower you. Once you push through and take that first step, momentum begins to build. One step leads to a second, and then a third, creating a ripple effect of progress. Think of it like trying to move a stationary vehicle in neutral. At first, it may appear impossible to shift the weight of the whole car. Yet, once the wheels start turning, the momentum carries it forward.

You begin to feel an exhilarating sense of achievement, and each day unfolds as a new opportunity to push your metaphorical car—an energizing prospect that cultivates self-created momentum. Before long, this process becomes ingrained in your daily routine. The parameters you initially set for yourself start to fade into the background, overshadowed by the excitement of growth and achievement. You begin to crave this newfound energy and momentum, anticipating all the possibilities that lie ahead. So, let that be your guiding principle. When the desire to give in or hold back surfaces, draw upon that fire within you to propel yourself forward. Embrace the challenge, as each step you take is a testament to your resilience and determination.

Remember, the only limits that exist are the ones you impose on yourself. It's time to break free from those constraints, reclaim your narrative, and move onward and upward toward the life you envision. The journey may not always be easy, but with every small victory, you are paving the way to a future filled with endless potential.

With all that said, I want to be profoundly transparent about one crucial truth: you will never reach the finish line without first making your way to the start line. It may sound simple, yet this foundational step is often more challenging than it appears. Get your feet on the ground and take that first step, putting one foot in front of the other.

It's a straightforward concept, right? Not really. Millions, if not billions of individuals around the world find themselves unable or unwilling to rise from the comfort of their couches, even when they desperately want to. Why? Because they allow themselves to engage in conversations with that nagging little voice inside their heads, echoing discouraging thoughts like, "You're not worthy," or "You don't belong."

Now is the time to silence that voice and eradicate any form of disbelief that stems from these internal whispers. It's imperative to confront and fight those mental battles, transforming them into opportunities for victory every single day. Each morning when your alarm clock sounds, consider it a call to arms, a chance to battle for what is rightfully yours. Seize that moment!

Those who lack resilience may opt to take days off when conditions aren't ideal, but champions—the iron-willed—rise with enthusiasm and determination, ready to conquer the challenges before them and build the momentum needed to win the day.

Every time you succeed in winning these small battles, you inch closer to winning more days. And with each victory, more opportunities will naturally unfold. There's no magic trick or hidden power that will create the internal strength necessary to manifest your dreams. The essence of success lies in your ability to tap into personal, self-induced momentum whenever you need it, regardless of the challenges you face.

To achieve greatness, you must claim each moment and hold yourself accountable for putting in the work—performing those repetitive actions until they become ingrained in your identity. Anyone who has ever pushed through adversity to find success has mastered the art of generating their own momentum at will. They have repeatedly tested the boundaries of their comfort zones, allowing them to dig deep and unearth strength whenever needed.

There's a common adage suggesting it takes sixty-six days to form a habit. I propose a different perspective: it only takes one day—and that day is today. Regardless of whether you read this on a Monday or a Thursday, the opportunity to create a habit starts today. Are you ready and willing to commit to performing the same actions repeatedly today, understanding that this effort can reshape the trajectory of the rest of your life? It's time to transform that desire into action. The choice is yours.

Each decision you make today has the potential to lay the groundwork for the future you envision. Remember, every monumental achievement begins with a single step, and today is the day to take yours. Let that realization ignite a fire within you to act, to push forward, and to break through the barriers that have held you back for far too long. Embrace the process, and step boldly into the journey of your transformation. Your future self will thank you for it!

LIFE

In 2015, I made the decision to sign up for the Buffalo Half-Marathon, a choice that would set the stage for remarkable transformation. At that time, I was navigating a whirlwind of responsibilities: teaching full-time, pursuing my Master's degree from Canisius College, coaching varsity softball, and planning my wedding for that fall. Looking back, it's a wonder how I managed to juggle everything.

Each of us faces our own busy lives, and it's all too easy to spin a narrative that excuses us from taking action. We often allow ourselves to engage in negotiations with that internal voice, and more often than not, that voice wins the debate. That persistent inner dialogue leads to thoughts such as, "It's too hard," "You're too sore," or "You're too tired."

It becomes far too simple to concoct excuses that justify remaining inactive instead of getting on your feet and taking meaningful action. The list of reasons for inaction stretches endlessly, but when you allow yourself to sidestep your commitments, you are being disloyal to your future. You're shortchanging your dreams and aspirations. Consider how you would feel if you had a friend who continuously promised to help you but never followed through.

Picture this: every Saturday, they assure you they'll come over to assist you with that long-overdue appliance installation. You need a partner's hands to finish the task, yet weekend after weekend, your friend fails to show up at 10 AM as promised. The time rolls by, and you're left waiting, all while believing in their words.

Don't be that unreliable friend to yourself. Stop making promises that you inevitably break, only to fall into the trap of excuses. It takes no courage to take the easy way out and not deliver; however, that's not who you are. Each morning, you will undoubtedly wake up with some aches and pains. Perhaps you'll spend the first fifteen minutes contemplating your existence and whether or not to simply stay in bed. But upon opening your eyes to the sound of your alarm clock, remind yourself that every moment is a precious gift. Life itself is a treasure, and every day grants you another opportunity to rise up and fight once again.

To overcome the hurdles of daily life, it's crucial to recognize that existence often resembles a battle. The sooner you accept that life's challenges require strategic effort, the quicker you can thwart the constant internal negotiations that arise each morning. Make a promise to yourself that on each day that you can place two feet firmly on the ground, you will rise and take a small risk. You will resolve to take that first step—whatever that may look like for you—and activate the momentum that will drive you forward.

Initially, these small "reps" may feel insignificant, but they will soon evolve into more substantial actions and eventually lead to sets of progress that propel you forward. All of a sudden, you will find yourself so deeply focused on your journey that the doubts and conversations that once held you back fade away. You will discover a newfound craving for the work ahead. You'll fall in love with the process—the sweat, the effort, the journey of becoming who you aspire to be. This is where you need to be. This is where you deserve to be. Embrace the struggle, honor your commitments, and commit to showing up for yourself every single day. Each moment you invest in your personal growth compounds over time, building the extraordinary life you envision. So, take that first step, break free from the chains of indecision, and step boldly into the purpose-driven life waiting for you.

It was the spring of 2015, a time filled to the brim with commitments and aspirations. I was immersed in my work, diligently pursuing my Master's degree, training for a half marathon, and dedicated to building a competitive softball team. Balancing these demanding projects was no easy feat, yet I understood that each day required active engagement in my thoughts and unwavering commitment to my intentions. I had made promises to myself, and I knew I had to follow through.

Looking back, I can't recall a single day during that whirlwind season of my life where I allowed myself the luxury of taking a break or a moment to let my mental and physical guards down. It felt as though every waking hour was a race against time, driven by deadlines and objectives that seemed to multiply as I tackled them. But in those moments of intensity—and yes, sometimes exhaustion—I uncovered a profound truth. These periods of relentless effort are often the best teachers of resilience, adaptability, and determination.

The urgency of that time in my life taught me one crucial lesson. There is always a path forward if we are willing to seek it. When we commit ourselves to our goals and actively engage with our challenges, we develop the capacity to forge our own paths, even when obstacles threaten to deter us.

In striving for excellence, whether academically, athletically, or personally, we are often pushed to our limits. It is precisely during these demanding times that we learn to tap into our inner strength and capabilities. I discovered that the more I dedicated myself to these pursuits, the more I honed my ability to adapt, plan, and execute effectively.

Each challenge became a stepping stone, replete with opportunities for growth and learning. In the same vein, we can all find ourselves in a similar position, juggling multiple responsibilities and chasing after dreams that may seem daunting. But if you keep your focus locked on your goals and maintain that commitment, even amid the chaos, you'll be surprised by how far you can go.

So, as you move forward in your own life, remember that those moments of struggle and hard work are not hindrances but rather significant components of your journey. Embrace the challenges, stay engaged with your goals, and trust in your ability to persist, even when the odds seem stacked against you. It's through this determination and focus that you will prove to yourself, time and time again, that there is always a way forward, and that you have everything within you to succeed. Take a look at THIS schedule!!

4:30 am: **Master's Program Grad**

 Homework Assignments

5:30 am: **Read for 30 Minutes**

6:30 am: **Leave for School**

7:15 am: **Master's Program and Daily Preparation**

7:30 – 3:15 pm: **School**

3:30 – 5:30 pm: **Softball Practice**

5:30 – 6:30/7:30 pm: **Marathon Training**

8:00 pm: **Home and Wedding Planning**

IRONMAN

The day I signed up for the Maryland Ironman was a turning point in my life, filled with an overwhelming sense of ecstasy. Joy and excitement flooded my being as I shared the news that

I had taken on the monumental challenge of a full Ironman with everyone around me. I quickly texted my family, posted a vibrant announcement on social media, and felt as though I was ready to conquer the world. Yet paradoxically, I had no real understanding of what an Ironman entails. What I did have at that moment was unbridled enthusiasm, and that alone fueled my determination to get started.

The first five days of training were nothing short of phenomenal. I was meticulously hydrating myself, logging my running miles, incorporating regular stretching sessions, and even getting on my bike from time to time. I had a swimming strategy that I believed would set me on the path to success, at least, that's what I thought at the time.

However, it's fascinating how easily that initial thrill can evaporate. The excitement, like a candle burning late into the night, is a temporary high that inevitably dims. As the days went on and my energy waned, I found myself grappling with the emptiness that would often follow such periods of enthusiasm.

In those moments, it's common to search for temporary fixes, filling the void with physical items such as new watches or fancy shoes. But, just as quickly as that excitement ignites, these material possessions also lose their luster over time. When you find yourself at a crossroads, where happiness feels unattainable and creating motivation seems impossible, it's crucial to take control immediately. This is often a challenging concept to grasp, particularly in moments of hesitation when your mind feels like it's in a whirlwind. This is precisely the time to dig deep and grind through the doubt.

Refusing to succumb to self-doubt is essential. When those insidious thoughts creep in, whispering that you should take a day off or hit the snooze button one more time, you must summon the determination to push back and discover that next surge of energy.

Consider what happens when you convince yourself that one day doesn't matter or that it's fine to let this one slip by. Each time you allow that mindset to take root, it becomes easier and easier to quit in the long run. Over time, we grow numb to the notion of giving up or failing. We start seeking comfort in fleeting pleasures and immediate gratifications, which ultimately leads us down a slippery slope, stripping away our sense of purpose and direction.

This realization, that we are making choices based on transient feelings rather than long-term goals, can be profound. Each hasty decision nudges us further away from the straight path of growth and expansion. It's crucial to never allow yourself to reach that point of complacency. While one day may seem insignificant in the grand scheme of things, each time you tell yourself, "It's just one day," you are paving the way for a series of "just one days." Each small surrender chips away at your progress and tempts you deeper into the abyss of complacency and loss.

As you descend into this cycle, the pressure mounts, making it seem increasingly impossible to pull yourself out of the trap you've created for yourself. The key is to act now—to take decisive steps and commit to your goals without looking back. Remember, the victories we achieve in small, consistent increments build the foundation for monumental success. Embrace the grind and trust in your ability to push through the discomfort.

By doing so, you set yourself on a path toward lasting achievement and fulfillment. So, when doubt whispers in your ear, drown it out with your determination. Forge ahead, and don't let momentary setbacks sway you from your course. You are capable of more than you realize, and every step you take—no matter how small—means you are that much closer to the life you aspire to lead. Choose to rise above today, and you'll not only strengthen your resolve but also pave the way for a brighter and more fulfilled tomorrow.

For our spring break in April 2022, my family and I packed up my truck and set off in search of warmer temperatures. We had reserved a charming beach house in Destin, Florida, positioned right on the shore, promising us a week of sun and relaxation. Our journey began under less than ideal circumstances, nevertheless, as we left behind a blizzard that blanketed the region in a fierce whiteout. The storm seemed to trail us throughout the first half of our trip, yet we pressed on, fueled by our anticipation of blue skies and sandy beaches. Finally, after what felt like an endless expedition, we reached our vacation rental late on Saturday night.

When Sunday morning dawned, I woke to the soothing sounds of waves crashing against the rocks and the beautiful golden sun rising over the horizon. It was a surreal welcome, and I knew I had the opportunity to embrace both family time and the relaxed atmosphere of Destin. While I had planned a long run for that Sunday as part of my training regimen, I decided to prioritize the experience with my loved ones and push my run back by a day, recognizing the importance of balance.

After spending the day basking in the sun, absorbing the warmth of the sea salt and the laughter of my family, it was time to shift my mindset and prepare myself for the three-hour run that awaited me. Throughout the day, I diligently chugged over a gallon of water, knowing that staying hydrated was crucial, especially under the relentless sun. Yet, it seemed that no matter how much I drank, the sun thirstily claimed it all back. I made every effort to hydrate and fuel my body, fully aware that my performance would depend on it.

Following the near accident on the road, you can feel the despair and pain. Onward and upward.
Barmore Photo Collection

As we closed the day with a delightful dinner filled with laughter, I took a moment to shower off the sand that clung to my skin and rinse away the greasy remnants of sunscreen. Standing under the high-pressure hot water, I felt invigorated with each splash, a reminder that Monday would soon arrive and I had to be prepared for the challenge ahead and right away, I realized I had slipped into vacation mode, and my training had momentarily lost its priority in my thoughts. This recognition sparked a realization. I needed to tap into my inner resolve, my inner Hyde, if you will.

It's not uncommon to experience moments when your energy and focus begin to wane, particularly during times of indulgence or relaxation. These are the moments when you must actively engage your "Hyde" side, the part of you that is relentless and driven to push through. The story of Dr. Jekyll and Mr. Hyde is a classic tale of a well-respected scientist who grapples with his dual nature. In his quest for separation between his good and dark sides, he concocts a potion that allows him to embody both extremes.

Similarly, we all possess the capacity for both pleasure and discipline, and there are times when we must embrace that inner tenacity to conquer challenges, especially when life attempts to distract us from our goals. As I prepared for my run the following day, I reminded myself that recognizing the need for balance and discipline is a vital part of the journey. Just like Dr. Jekyll, I had to acknowledge both facets of my existence to find harmony—with the eagerness to savor vacation while simultaneously honoring my commitment to training.

As you embark on your own journeys, remember that there will be times of indulgence and relaxation, and there will also be moments that require discipline and focus. Embrace both parts of yourself, but never lose sight of your ultimate goals. Tap into that inner force, channel the relentless energy within you, and remember, it's never too late to shift your mindset and recommit to your aspirations. Each moment is an opportunity to choose action over inertia, to chase your dreams while also indulging in the beauty of life around you.

The key is to find harmony and propel yourself forward, no matter where you are on your journey. You are capable of achieving greatness. All it takes is the willingness to embrace both sides of your nature and the determination to keep moving ahead. When Dr. Jekyll consumed the potion, he unleashed a second personality, Mr. Hyde. Hyde represents Jekyll's savage alter ego, embodying all of his primal instincts and base desires.

While on vacation, I found myself embracing the spirit of Dr. Jekyll, allowing myself to enjoy life to the fullest. With that being said, there comes a time when I need to make the necessary shift and harness my inner Hyde, pushing aside frivolities to focus on my goals. Fortunately, I was able to cultivate a powerful internal dialogue that prioritized the tasks I genuinely valued over momentary pleasures. Nevertheless, that night was far from restful.

My dreams morphed into nightmares, a reflection of my racing thoughts filled with anxieties about the upcoming challenges. Images of long roads along the beach and the notion of warm temperatures flooded my mind. I found myself grappling with the uncertainties that loomed ahead. The path I would travel and the terrain I would encounter were unknowns that left me feeling apprehensive. Answers for these questions remained elusive, tantalizingly out of reach as I drifted in and out of consciousness. When the alarm clock rang violently at 3:30 AM, it jolted me awake, serving as an unmistakable reminder that it was time for Dr. Jekyll to step aside and let Hyde take control. I needed to channel that inner strength and determination to face the day ahead. I quickly prepared a small breakfast, opting for a refreshing Gatorade—an orange one, of course—and chugged down a few good sips of water.

You might be wondering why orange Gatorade specifically. The truth is, there's no profound explanation behind it. It's my favorite flavor. If I'm going to fuel my body, I want it to taste good.

As I hit the road by 5:00 AM, I was graced by minimal traffic, a blessing that allowed me to enjoy a peaceful start before the inevitable stampede of vacationers descended upon the area. The temperature felt just right, perfect for an early morning run. I removed my headphones initially, reveling in the natural symphony of birds chirping in the trees and the rhythmic sound of waves crashing onto the shore. It was a moment of tranquility that set a positive tone for the journey ahead.

Nonetheless, as I continued down the asphalt path, the road began to narrow, the temperature steadily rising, and the traffic began to thicken. An unsettling realization struck me. I was ill-prepared. For the first time in my training, I had set out without sufficient water or food. I had about thirty minutes to cover enough distance before I would need to turn back home. With each passing mile, my anxiety intensified as jacked-up monster trucks zoomed past me with little regard for my presence on the road.

As I reached the tenth mile, a sense of unease washed over me, prompting me to glance over my shoulder. At that exact moment, an alarming realization hit me. The mirror of a lifted F-250 brushed alarmingly close to my arm. I felt a rush of adrenaline mixed with fear, a reminder of the risks that accompany not only physical challenges but also the personal journeys we undertake.

This experience was a vivid illustration of the importance of preparation and the necessity of listening to that inner voice of caution. In life, whether you are training for an Ironman or pursuing any other grand ambition, it's essential to strike a balance between the excitement of the journey and the practical realities that come with it. Embrace the unpredictability of your path, but don't lose sight of the fundamental preparations that guide you toward success.

Whether you're training, planning, or pursuing a dream, stay committed to your goals and ensure you are equipped with what you need to navigate the obstacles ahead. Remember, every journey you undertake is filled with valuable lessons. Embrace them, learn from them, and let them propel you forward. So, as you lace up your shoes and step out onto your path, take a moment to reflect on the preparation that fuels your journey, and let the drive from within lead you toward your achievements, one determined step at a time.

It was in that juncture that I felt as though a torrent of emotions surged through my mind, colliding with one another in a chaotic wave. I was angry, sad, bitter, and downright scared. The determined, fearless side of me, my inner Hyde, seemed to evaporate as I stopped my run to regather my thoughts and refocus on the task at hand. I made my way down toward the beach, all the while steering myself in the right direction toward the halfway point of my journey.

As I walked, I concentrated on what needed to be done, bringing back to the forefront of my mind the commitment I had made. With each unsteady step, I felt myself wobbling as I approached the asphalt. I stood on the rumble strips, peering down the hazy path ahead, and took that first step. Then I followed it up with another, and then another. 'Focus on each step,' I reminded myself. 'Don't quit.'

My once-vibrant flame of motivation had dwindled to a mere glimmer, but I knew it was time to ignite the high-octane energy within me and reignite that passion. So that's precisely what I set out to do. I removed my headphones, allowing myself to fully embrace my surroundings. Though I feared the distractions posed by vacationers and busy locals, I chose to prioritize my own well-being and focus.

Energized by the sense of control returning to me, I approached the halfway mark with determination and even pushed a little further than I had anticipated. I found myself on a high, refusing to succumb to the obstacles that threatened to engulf me from all angles. This experience was one of my most significant victories that spring, as I resolutely refused to let external influences tarnish what I needed to accomplish.

Following the near-accident alongside the road that day, it would have been all too easy to dial Adrienne and tell her that I was done with my run and needed a ride home. Instead, I made a conscious, calculated decision to dismiss every excuse that crept into my head that morning and replaced it with action.

Each time we discover a way to persevere in the face of uncertainty, we sharpen our mental toughness and cultivate resilience to our advantage. The stronger we become mentally, the greater the momentum we create to withstand the unpredictable challenges that life throws our way. It's perfectly normal to think about quitting. Sometimes even contemplating giving up is part of the process. Even still, at the end of the day, despite all adversity or hardship you face, you must convince yourself that there is no other way to reach the final stroke of your masterpiece than to navigate directly through the most resistant paths imaginable.

Remember, each journey begins with a single step, and every step counts. One step, one repetition, one day, and one week at a time will propel you toward destinations that once felt like distant dreams. As you embark on your own journey, recognize that it is the small, consistent actions taken over time that lead to monumental achievements. Embrace the process, fight through the discomfort, and trust in your ability to overcome. Your path may be laden with challenges, but every hurdle you conquer will shape you into the person you are meant to be.

I was beginning to gain strength and confidence.
This was a week out from Cambridge.
Barmore Photo Collection

REFLECTION

1. What is ONE goal that you are currently working towards?

   a. _____

2. What is one roadblock that may be holding you back from reaching this goal?

   _____

   _____

   _____

   _____

3. Have you ever overcome a fear? What was it? How did you do it?

   _____

   _____

   _____

   _____

CHAPTER 6

BE FEROCIOUS

At some point during my journey, I encountered a thought-provoking idea within the pages of a book that stated, "The harder you push, the happier you will become."

This concept can be quite challenging to fully grasp, primarily because we often construct an idealized image of happiness that doesn't seem to correlate with pushing ourselves to our limits. When we picture happiness, we might envision Snoop Dog lounging on a sun-drenched beach, sipping a Corona. While this idyllic scene may represent the ultimate relaxation to many, it's crucial to understand that such moments of comfort seldom lead to sustained bliss or fulfillment.

Let's take a moment to engage in a brief mental exercise. I encourage you to close your eyes for a few seconds and reflect on the last time you accomplished something extraordinarily difficult. I'm not referring to the everyday tasks like doing the dishes or folding laundry. I'm talking about those moments that truly challenged you, perhaps when you completed a long-distance run, tackled a complex project, or even pieced together a 1,000-piece puzzle all by yourself. Can you remember a specific event in your life that tested your limits, yet, through exceptional effort, you achieved the outcome you had envisioned?

Now, ask yourself this: Did that experience bring you a sense of joy? I can confidently say that for most people, the answer will be a resounding yes. If you're thinking otherwise, you might be lying to yourself or simply haven't tapped into the profound depths of what your body and mind can endure. Sure, the journey may have been fraught with struggle and discomfort every step of the way, but we can collectively agree that those experiences of physical and mental challenge contribute significantly to our overall sense of happiness and fulfillment.

Consider this: Every self-induced acute stressor that you intentionally welcome into your life serves as a catalyst for transforming the way you approach and seek out happiness. There's certainly a time and a place for leisurely activities, like lounging on the beach with a chilled drink in hand, but these moments should not overshadow your relentless pursuit of your wildest dreams.

True joy often resides on the other side of discomfort. It lies in the grind of pushing yourself beyond your comfort zone and embracing the more intense aspects of your personality—what I refer to as your inner Hyde. While doubt may rear its head and try to steer you away from taking action, it's essential to pursue the most challenging path when faced with decisions at the critical forks in the road. Each tough choice and every grueling workout will lead you to a land of prosperity and achievement that you wholeheartedly deserve. The accolades and accomplishments you gather along the way will affirm that the grind has been worth it. Ultimately, isn't that what life is all about?

Each experience, each victory, and each hard-fought battle

crafts your story, a story that you hold the pen to. As the author of your life, make it a good one. Embrace the challenges, seek out the discomfort, and push yourself harder than you ever thought possible. By doing so, you will not only discover the depths of your true potential but also create a life rich with meaning, purpose, and, yes, happiness. Remember, the struggle is not just an obstacle; it's a vital part of your journey towards becoming the person you aspire to be. Make each day count, and turn that potential into reality!

LIFE

When reflecting on my journey to transform my average life into an Iron Life, it's impossible to overlook the profound impact my brother, Brian, has had on my perspective and my path. He has been a trailblazer in our family, reshaping my understanding of what it means to truly live.

Brian embodies adventure and exploration, constantly seeking experiences that ignite enthusiasm for life. His spirit has paved the way for me to redefine my own aspirations. On April 21, 2019, Brian laced up his hiking boots in Campo, California, and fixed his gaze north. He was on the cusp of attempting one of the world's most iconic treks: the Pacific Crest Trail. Spanning from Mexico to Canada, this remarkable journey is one that fewer than 10,000 people have completed. When I refer to Brian as the pioneer in our family, I am emphasizing how he transformed everything I believed was possible. Before Brian's adventures, I never thought it was feasible to explore the world in the way he did. Yet, I learned that he has set foot on six out of the seven continents, embracing curiosity and adventure with a zeal that was both inspiring and infectious.

I also believed that running a marathon was an unattainable goal, but once again, Brian proved me wrong when he completed his first marathon in under four hours. His dedication and tenacity shattered my misconceptions about physical limits and endurance. Brian's adventures didn't stop at marathons. He's attended the Olympics, cheered at playoff football games, and even hopped on a plane to fly across the country for a one-night concert. He epitomizes the essence of spontaneity and adventure. Remarkably, even though he is younger than I am, Brian has always been a figure I admire and look up to. His relentless pursuit of experiences has encouraged me to step outside my comfort zone and embrace my own potential.

As Brian stood at the border of Mexico and the United States, with only 2,653 miles of rugged trail stretching before him, his singular focus was clear: FINISH! This unwavering determination exemplified not only his goal for that journey but also served as a life lesson for me and anyone else who dreams of achieving greatness. Brian's pursuit teaches us that it's not merely about setting a goal. It's about embracing the journey, understanding the challenges that lie ahead, and maintaining the resilience to push through them. His adventures remind us that life is a canvas waiting to be painted with our dreams, aspirations, and unyielding spirit. In essence, let Brian's example serve as a beacon of inspiration for you as you embark on your own journey toward self-improvement and fulfillment.

Brian finishing the Pacific Crest Trail. Once again, my inspiration.
Barmore Photo Collection

Understand that the limits you perceive are often self-imposed. Choose to redefine your possibilities and set your sights on the extraordinary. Just like Brian, when faced with the daunting question of "how," the answer lies within your readiness to commit to that bold ambition and take the first step forward. Embrace the adventure ahead, for the journey will shape you in ways you have yet to imagine!

If you've never challenged yourself with something

extraordinarily difficult—like enduring a long-distance run, training for a physique competition, tackling a complex puzzle, or hiking the Pacific Crest Trail—you may be missing out on some of life's most enriching experiences. Yet here's the silver lining about missing out. Until the "final call" arrives, you still have the power to rewrite your own script.

As T.S. Eliot wisely said, "Only by reaching so far do we discover how far it is possible to go."

Take my brother, Brian, for example. When he embarked on his ambitious trek from the United States-Mexico border to the Canadian border, he had no guarantee of survival along the way. However, he had already embraced discomfort as a teacher, and through this experience, he tapped into the essence of what it feels like to seek and achieve the extraordinary. Each day brought a fresh wave of radical adversity. He faced challenges from the wildlife lurking in the wilderness, unpredictable weather patterns, and the harsh realities of rugged trail conditions. There were moments when he didn't possess the right strategies or made decisions that resulted in unforeseen difficulties, but that unpredictability is often the most thrilling aspect of any adventure. Yes, he encountered his share of rough days—experiencing both literal and figurative peaks and valleys, as we all do.

The true distinction that separates those who reach the pinnacle of their ambitions from those who hover at the base is often the ability to adapt and evolve. It is essential to understand that failure and mistakes are not merely setbacks. They are vital components of growth and learning.

Brian lived this truth firsthand as he ventured off the beaten path toward Mount Whitney, a formidable summit that few would even dare to contemplate. Standing tall at 14,505 feet,

Whitney is the highest peak in the contiguous United States, and depending on the season, it can present extreme dangers. Blazing through a blizzard, navigating deep snow, and summiting the peak posed significant challenges that tested Brian's limits.

On more than one occasion during this treacherous journey, he found himself confronted with the very real fear for his life. I vividly remember a moment when he called our Dad, expressing the raw vulnerability of uncertainty—he didn't know if he would make it back alive.

Such experiences embody the essence of personal growth. They remind us that life is rife with challenges, but it is through facing these challenges head-on that we forge our strength and discover our true capabilities. Embracing discomfort and adversity allows us to stretch beyond our previous boundaries, ultimately leading to greater fulfillment and understanding of not just our surroundings, but of ourselves.

So, if you find yourself on the sidelines of life, hesitant to engage in challenges that could lead to profound growth, I urge you to reconsider. Grab hold of the opportunity to step outside your comfort zone. Set audacious goals and pursue them with fervor. The challenges you take on, like the peaks you climb, are not simply obstacles. They are stepping stones to a richer, more meaningful existence.

Remember, adventure awaits, and by daring to journey beyond the familiar, you will uncover not just your potential but also the transformative power of resilience and determination. Embrace the journey, welcome the struggles, and recognize that every peak conquered adds to the tapestry of your unique story. Your adventure begins now—make it one worth remembering!

The conditions were almost unbearable, but as he stood

triumphantly at the summit of his magical hike, he took a picture. This was not just any photograph. It is one that will forever be etched in my memory. In that image, he wore a smile so wide it seemed to stretch 2,653 miles, radiating joy and fulfillment. The sparkle in his eyes mirrored the triumph of having pushed through some of the harshest elements that nature could muster. At that moment, the vision he had painstakingly crafted in his mind came to life in a vibrant display of achievement.

After completing the arduous climb, I asked him what his favorite part of the entire expedition had been. Without a moment's hesitation, he declared that it was his battle with Mount Whitney. This trek, which could have represented a formidable endpoint for many, emerged as the most unforgettable and cherished segment of his remarkable journey. He had captured that pivotal photograph at the pinnacle of Whitney, not just as a keepsake, but as irrefutable proof that he had made it.

The image served as both a celebration of his accomplishment and a reminder that even if he hadn't returned to the beaten path, he had fulfilled his promise to himself and us all. This experience reinforces a powerful truth: All great achievements arise from the willingness to tap into our wild side, embodying ferocity in our actions until we reach the goals we set for ourselves.

It's essential that we don't allow ourselves to take the easy way out simply due to a self-imposed notion of what happiness should look like or feel like. Rather, we should strive to do something extraordinarily difficult that pushes us out of our comfort zones and invites discomfort and distress into our lives. Now, does this mean you need to climb Mount Whitney or compete in an Ironman? Absolutely not.

The essence of what constitutes *hard* varies significantly from person to person. Everyone has their unique challenges to face. The key is to ask yourself what you truly value. What goals are you passionate about pursuing? From there, commit to that vision and refuse to stop until you've attained it. Following through and completing the objectives you set can provoke profound feelings of satisfaction and empowerment. There's a transformative power in finishing what you began, and that sense of accomplishment can resonate deeply within you. When you push past the obstacles and barriers that seek to hold you back, you will not only gain insight into your true capabilities but will also experience a newfound resilience that can influence every aspect of your life. So, take that next step, embracing the challenges that lie ahead.

Whether it's reaching for a lofty goal or conquering a personal obstacle, hold on to your vision and see it through. Each moment spent persevering is a testament to your character and determination. The journey is as important as the destination. Relish each step you take, and allow those experiences, like the unforgettable image my brother captured, to inspire you as you continue on your path toward personal greatness.

IRONMAN

Preparing for a challenge as monumental as training for an Ironman can be likened to tackling a towering margarita served in one of those gigantic glasses at a fancy Mexican restaurant. It's a daunting task, one that demands not just commitment but an unwavering resolve to push beyond the limits.

I quickly realized that I could not perform at my best unless I infused every aspect of my training with relentless effort. The word "relentless" typically defines an oppressively constant and incessant pursuit of something meaningful. Be that as it may, maintaining this level of consistency in your actions can become incredibly frustrating over time. It requires a fierce, almost aggressive attitude, a trait that only a handful of individuals manage to embody fully.

If you aspire to pursue a significant goal—whatever that may be—it's crucial to remind yourself regularly of the need to be fierce and undeterred. There are no alternatives when it comes to executing your daily practices. You must cultivate a merciless determination. It is easy to become overwhelmed by the magnitude of the ultimate goal, but rather than fixating on the end product or the finish line, shift your focus to the journey ahead. You will never reach the finish line by simply daydreaming about it. Instead, embrace the process and commit to conquering each day, one objective at a time.

Every single day brings a new opportunity to advance toward your goal, and it's vital to approach these days with the enthusiasm and vigor that a new adventure deserves. Get to the start line of each day with that same excitement that propels you forward. By concentrating on the present moment, you'll maximize your efforts and increase your chances of success. It's important to break down the daunting task at hand into manageable chunks, allowing yourself to celebrate the small victories that come with every completed day.

Remember, running a marathon of any sort, be it physical or emotional, is about pacing yourself, maintaining focus, and taking it step by step. Each small achievement builds upon itself, gradually leading you closer to your ultimate destination. Embrace the relentless effort required to forge ahead. Develop a mentality that thrives on the everyday challenges and reaffirm your commitment in those moments when frustration threatens to derail your progress. Cultivating this fierce mindset will not only help propel you through rigorous training and daunting challenges but will also foster resilience in every aspect of your life.

As you continue to tackle each day with ferocity and intent, you'll find that the sense of accomplishment you gain is not just about achieving the monumental goal but about mastering the art of relentless persistence. So, the next time you feel overwhelmed by the enormity of your aspirations, remember to focus on the journey rather than the destination.

Approach each day as a new start line, refueled with excitement, and commit to making progress. Your relentless pursuit will, undoubtedly, lead you to remarkable achievements and a deeper understanding of your incredible potential. The path may be challenging, but with each determined step, you create a legacy of effort, resilience, and triumph that far exceeds any single finish line.

Swimming emerged as my most significant challenge during my training, particularly following my near disaster in Chautauqua Lake. The experience left me grappling with an intense fear of the water, a considerable obstacle that loomed large in my mind. The swimming segment of the Ironman became the most daunting part of my training regimen, primarily because I struggled to limit distractions while navigating the vastness of open water.

*Training in the week leading up to the Ironman. This was the day I
started to truly believe I could do it.*
Barmore Photo Collection

Each time I entered the pool or the lake, I had to consciously
engage my body and mind with every stroke. I reminded myself
that to stay afloat and progress, I could not take a single stroke
for granted. When submerged, it's all too easy for your thoughts
to drift toward the finish line, resulting in a mental lapse that
can disrupt your focus. This is where many people falter. Their
minds begin to wander, and the descent into confusion starts.

If you allow yourself to fixate on completing the task ahead,
you risk losing control of your performance, undermining
everything you've worked so hard to accomplish. The mantra I
adopted became clear: Be present. Stay focused on what's right
in front of you. I understand that this is often easier said than
done, which is why I found meditation to be an invaluable

practice. The ability to control your thoughts is fundamental, and honing this skill can significantly enhance your concentration in every moment.

Each day before my training sessions, I would retreat to my basement, turn off the lights, and meditate for five to ten minutes. In those moments of stillness, I focused on my breathing, diligently blocking out the external noise and chaos of everyday life. While the physical demands of Ironman training were intense, the most challenging and revealing part of my daily routine was the meditation itself, as I wrestled with the task of quieting my mind amidst the chaos. Stepping away from the commotion of the world and turning inward provided me with a necessary respite. But I won't sugarcoat it. The early days of meditation were tough, they felt clumsy and ineffective.

Nevertheless, this struggle is a vital aspect of growth. It is in these challenging early moments that persistence is most crucial. You will likely experience failure, disappointment, and frustration. But remember, each attempt brings you one step closer to success. Eventually, after multiple attempts and a commitment to stay the course, I found solace and clarity during my meditative practice. I was able to calm my mind and remain present in the moment without succumbing to distractions.

With each passing day, as I fortified my mental resilience, I recognized dramatic improvements in my swimming, running, and cycling abilities. The most significant growth, however, was visible in my swimming. I discovered that I could maintain my concentration in challenging conditions: whether my goggles fogged up, I lost track of my position in the water, or if the lake was colder than I anticipated. Conditions that had previously derailed me no longer posed an issue. I was finally in control, and this crucial piece of mental fortitude was what I had been missing during the earlier weeks of my training.

The start signal rang out, and it was go time. It was my moment to shine as I plunged into the depths of the Choptank River. A wave of emotions surged through me, but I knew it wasn't the time to dwell on feelings. I needed to employ my mental tools to acclimate to my surroundings. Fifty yards into the water, I faced my first serious shock-both literally and figuratively. It was the anticipated jellyfish, and it stung me across the face. As I swiped at it to remove it, my goggles shifted. In that moment, I found myself at a crossroads. I could either pick myself up or succumb to defeat. You already know I only gave myself one choice: fix the goggles and move onward.

Then, a fellow athlete grabbed me, which startled me a bit. However, I was so immersed in the rhythm of my strokes that I refused to let it shake my focus. Stroke after stroke, I began to gain confidence, believing in myself more and more. Several jellyfish stings and unintentional swats at my feet later, I was approaching the beach. The long-awaited and most intimidating section of my Ironman was almost behind me.

If you aspire to be fierce and relentless in your pursuits, you must be willing to sharpen every tool in your arsenal. The development of mental toughness turned out to be the cornerstone for my transformation. It was the essential element that bridged the gap between an average existence and an Iron Life. By investing time in nurturing your mental strength, you unlock the potential to overcome the challenges that lie ahead.

So, embrace the discomfort, face the distractions, and commit to the process of refining your mind. In doing so, you will prepare yourself for greatness, be ready to conquer every challenge and achieve the dreams you hold dear.

REFLECTION

1. What is a "down the road" goal that you have? Something that you're not currently physically/mentally prepared for?

    a. _____

2. What is something that you are proud of from your past? WHY?

    _____

    _____

    _____

    _____

3. What is something you fear? NOT BEARS, NOT SNAKES, NOT SPIDERS. Something that you fear that will create growth in your life.

    _____

    _____

    _____

    _____

CHAPTER 7

P – P

PATIENCE

Three days before Christmas in 2020, I found myself in a predicament that many can relate to—I forgot to order my wife's stocking stuffers. In a moment of desperation, I quickly hopped on Amazon, selected ten items, added them to my cart, and clicked the purchase button. At no point did it occur to me that my order might not arrive before the holiday. In today's fast-paced world, we have been conditioned to expect instant gratification. With services like DoorDash, Instacart, and Amazon Prime, we have been led to believe that we can have what we want with minimal thought or effort.

This convenience can trick us into thinking that acquiring the quality values in life—true fulfillment, growth, and lasting impact—comes with the same ease. This notion couldn't be further from the truth. If you genuinely want to leave a meaningful mark on the world and create a positive legacy, you must cultivate a different mindset, one that embodies patience and persistence.

To illustrate this point, consider the movement of a glacier. A glacier may only inch forward a mere inch or two each year, yet its relentless progress carves out immense valleys and shapes entire landscapes over time. This slow but steady transformation serves as a metaphor for the impact we can make in our own lives and in the lives of others. Just like the glacier, the path to achieving significant change may seem slow and arduous, but it is the consistent effort and commitment that leads to profound results.

Real transformation in life requires us to become masters of performing monotonous tasks, embracing the daily grind even when it feels tedious or exhausting. It's easy to get caught up in the allure of immediate results, but cultivating resilience and perseverance is essential for implementing lasting metamorphosis. Every small task you undertake contributes to your overall growth, and the cumulative effect of consistent effort is far more powerful than any quick fix.

When faced with challenges, remember that enduring change often requires you to take lessons from nature and commit to your journey with the same tenacity as a glacier. So, the next time you feel tempted to seek shortcuts or quick solutions, pause and reflect on the true nature of achievement. Understand that each step you take, no matter how small, is a vital part of a much larger journey. Embrace the process and reward yourself for the commitment to doing the hard work, even the monotonous tasks—because it is within those tasks that you shape your own legacy, inching ever closer to the greatness that you aspire to achieve.

The journey may be slow, but with patience and dedication, you can carve out a lasting impact in your life and in the lives of those around you. Most people approach their journey with the ferocity of a tornado, plowing through challenges with relentless speed. Yes, they often see significant change, but that change can be so overwhelming and chaotic that it may feel as if it is irreversible. With that said, it's essential to understand that the debris and destruction left in the wake of a tornado can always be cleaned up, repaired, and rebuilt. If you genuinely want to make your mark on your journey toward personal and professional growth, you will inevitably need to master the art of slowing down in the face of adversity.

The path to true success is rarely straightforward. It may be the rockiest, roughest, and most pothole-filled road you ever navigate. Just when you think the tumultuous journey will evolve into a smooth, paved path, you are often met with another obstacle. Life is not designed to be a leisurely stroll down the yellow brick road. Rather, it is a rugged terrain that will demand your blood, sweat, and tears. Every step and turn you take will test your resilience, and every challenge you face will contribute to your character development. Upon reaching the peak of your expedition, you will have the opportunity to look back at all the battles you overcame and feel immense gratitude for the lessons learned along the way. Those who remain patient and are willing to embrace the difficulties of their journey are often rewarded with meaningful growth.

Every setback, every difficult decision made, and each moment of struggle will impart invaluable lessons that serve to guide you toward success in the grander scheme of life. Conversely, those who lack patience and attempt to cut corners in pursuit of a quick solution will inevitably falter. When they encounter setbacks, they are often the first to point fingers and blame external circumstances, failing to take responsibility for their actions. They may rush to switch strategies or take shortcuts, only to find themselves trapped in a stale, mediocre existence, the very life they were striving to escape.

Understanding that exercising patience is actually how you speed up your progress may seem counterintuitive. Yet, in the journey toward any destination, time and space must be traversed. By cultivating patience, you'll find that you will arrive at your goals more effectively and meaningfully. On the other hand, cutting corners can lead to a situation where your ultimate destination slips further and further out of reach. Embrace the power of patience as an essential component of your journey. Accepting and nurturing this quality will enable you to make choices rooted in long-term success rather than fleeting gratification. It is in these moments of waiting and persevering that you develop strength, character, and clarity. So, take a deep breath, steady yourself, and remember: Real growth occurs over time as you navigate the uneven paths of your life's journey.

Embrace patience, for it is the true companion of achievement and fulfillment. As you hone this vital skill, you will find that the challenges you face today are simply stepping stones to the extraordinary future waiting for you. Make patience an essential part of everything you do. In any significant endeavor, you will encounter a multitude of individuals who bravely embark on their journeys. Many of them will inevitably face setbacks, finding themselves knocked down by the challenges life throws at them. Despite the feeling that I had, it is an unfortunate reality that only a few will muster the strength and determination to rise back up and make another attempt. Make it your mission to be one of those rare individuals who refuse to stay down.

When you experience defeat, don't abandon what you value simply because you've lost sight of your vision or feel overwhelmed by obstacles. It happens to everyone. There's no need to feel ashamed. Instead, take a moment to dig deep and search within yourself at all costs to reclaim what you once believed was attainable. Recognize that setbacks are rarely permanent unless you allow them to define your journey. Life is dynamic, and the road to success is often filled with bumps and detours. It is inevitable that we will slip up and stray off our intended path.

Embracing these moments of struggle is crucial because they provide invaluable opportunities for learning and development. When confronted with challenges, approach them with the understanding that not all victories come immediately. It's essential to remain steadfast, even when success seems tantalizingly out of reach. Always keep in mind that good things take time, and great things often require a little longer to achieve. Cultivating patience during these times will fortify your resilience, allowing you to persist through the trials.

As you journey toward your goals, remember to appreciate the small victories along the way. Each step you take, no matter how incremental, lays the foundation for future success. Instead of becoming disheartened by the difficulties you face, view each challenge as an opportunity to grow stronger. When you develop a mindset focused on patience and perseverance, you equip yourself with the tools needed to navigate any storm that comes your way.

Be intentional about fostering patience in all aspects of your life. Embrace the process, learn from your setbacks, and keep moving forward. With every new day, you have the chance to begin again, assured that your previous experiences serve as a guide to help you rise again. As you commit yourself to this mindset, you will not only conquer the challenges ahead but also emerge with a deeper understanding of yourself and what you are capable of achieving. Trust in the journey and remain patient, because success is not just a destination but a continual evolution of who you are becoming.

LIFE

I had the incredible privilege of coaching high school football for a decade, and during that time, I learned more than I could ever have hoped for. The last team I coached, the CSP Wolfpack, became a transformative experience for me as it allowed me to work alongside one of the best high school football coaches in New York State—Ty Harper.

Ty is a remarkable individual, a two-time New York State Championship winning head coach who was honored as Coach of the Year in 2018. Ty is not only an exceptional coach but also a good friend, and I owe much of my success, both in fitness and in life, to the way he carried himself, exemplifying patience and resilience. Watching him operate was enlightening, and I consciously sought to mirror his approach in my own endeavors.

Throughout our time together, I came to appreciate how his steadfast dedication ultimately shaped not only his teams but also the individuals within them. At any point, Ty could have chosen to veer off course or simply given in to the pressures surrounding him. Instead, he managed to transform a struggling 2-6 club into a back-to-back State Championship dynasty. His ability to adhere to a plan, to instill belief where others saw none, and to motivate our team to push beyond their limits taught me invaluable lessons about commitment and perseverance.

Ty's journey was a testament to the incredible power of resilience. He faced challenges head-on, demonstrating that obstacles could be turned into opportunities for growth. Every practice, every game, and every moment of doubt served as a building block in constructing a framework of success. The key takeaway from my experience with Ty is that no matter how daunting your goals may seem, discipline, patience, and an unwavering belief in your path can lead to extraordinary results.

It's essential to establish your vision and stay true to it, even when the winds of adversity threaten to throw you off course. Like Ty, embrace the challenges that come your way and use them as stepping stones toward achieving greatness. Remember, success isn't just about the outcome. It's also about the journey and how you conduct yourself along the way.

By applying the lessons I learned from Ty Harper, you can find the patience and resilience necessary to not only pursue your ambitions but to thrive amid the challenges that life presents. Harness the principles of dedication and commitment, and you, too, can transform your goals into reality, no matter how impossible they may initially seem. You just need to embody the same spirit and determination that you admire in those you look up to. Ultimately, it's this mindset that will guide you through the toughest of times and lead you to your own personal victory.

*Me and Coach Ty Harper circa 2018, the year of our State
Championship run.*
Barmore Photo Collection

In 2015, we embarked on an ambitious journey with high
hopes of transforming a first-year football team into an elite
force on the gridiron. Like any young coach, Ty exuded
enthusiasm and genuinely believed that we would achieve
immediate success. As the season unfolded, it became evident
that we were mistaken. Ty was wrong. I was wrong. We were all

wrong. We found ourselves on an unfortunate losing streak, enduring game after game without achieving a single victory.

Each contest was heart-wrenchingly close, as we faced off against established teams, but no matter how hard we fought, the elusive win remained out of our grasp. As the season concluded, we stood at a disappointing 2-6, grappling with our inability to find the answers we desperately sought. We felt we had the talent and the necessary tools to succeed, yet it seemed like we could never catch a break.

Despite this challenge, we decided to approach the summer of 2016 with a renewed mindset. We granted ourselves some grace for the underwhelming season we had just endured. We recognized that we had not met our own expectations. While we still aspired to achieve a winning record in the upcoming season, we committed to taking every practice seriously, never allowing ourselves to get too high on our accomplishments or too low on our failures. Grounded in our resolve, we understood that growth comes from learning from the past and maintaining a balanced perspective. When our schedule was released, we discovered that our first three games were against state-ranked opponents.

As the new season kicked off, we faced three demoralizing losses in quick succession. The stakes were high, and the pressure intensified with every setback. Yet through these trials, we began to cultivate resilience, understanding that true success is often forged in adversity. These early experiences served as vital lessons, reminding us that failure does not define us, it's how we respond to those failures that shapes our character and sets the stage for future victories. Each game was an opportunity to learn, refine our strategies, and grow stronger as a team. We knew the road ahead would be challenging, but we were determined to rise above our circumstances, to face every opponent with tenacity, and to transform the struggles of the past into stepping stones for a brighter future.

As you navigate your own path in life, whether through challenges in sports, work, or personal endeavors, remember that it's often the most difficult moments that offer the greatest potential for growth. Embrace the lessons embedded in setbacks, and maintain the resolve to keep pushing forward. Your journey may be bumpy and filled with obstacles, but with perseverance and an unwavering belief in your capabilities, you can shape your own narrative of success. Each step taken in the face of adversity brings you closer to achieving your dreams, no matter how unattainable they may seem at first. So, lace up your shoes, gather your courage, and get ready to redefine what's possible as you embark on your own extraordinary journey.

We may have let our chins dip and our heads hang low during those challenging times, but we were far from ready to give up. The following week, we faced another formidable opponent, and against the odds, we managed to sneak away with a hard-fought 20-15 victory, even after losing our star quarterback and team leader, Justin Svetz. His absence was a significant turning point for our squad. Svetz had been the glue that held our team together, embodying the spirit and tenacity that fueled our determination throughout the season.

In the face of adversity, a remarkable thing happened. Nolan Eggleston, our backup quarterback, stepped up courageously to lead our team to victory against a perennial powerhouse in our area. His resolve and ability to rally the team became the turning point we desperately needed. With this newfound momentum, we pushed forward, ultimately ending the season with a commendable record of 5-4. We even captured the title of "Best of the Rest" champion, a distinction given to the top team in the bottom half of the league. While it wasn't the championship we had aspired to, it signified the beginning of something greater on the horizon. The answers we had prayed for night after night were starting to materialize, guiding us out of the murky waters of uncertainty.

We began to experience a long-awaited pivot, moving from where we started to where we believed we should be. Anticipation for the upcoming 2017 season was at an all-time high, with a renewed sense of purpose and determination fueling our readiness to succeed. Upon receiving our schedule, we noted that our first few games were indeed winnable, and we couldn't wait to prove ourselves.

Our season opener was against a crosstown rival, a team we felt confident we were more talented than. Yet, during the first half, we found ourselves falling short on the scoreboard and trailing at halftime. Instead of letting our spirits falter or allowing doubt to creep in, we pulled ourselves together for an inspiring second half, ultimately sealing a resounding 45-20 victory.

When faced with challenges, it is essential to maintain your focus and rally your resilience, just as our team did. Each moment of adversity is an opportunity to learn, grow, and emerge stronger. As you progress in your own journey, remember that the most significant victories often follow periods of hardship.

In life, just as in sports, the ability to adapt, the courage to persevere, and the willingness to embrace change can lead you to achieve greatness. As you navigate your challenges, harness the momentum that comes from victories, no matter how small, and let it propel you toward your goals. Remember, it's not just about where you start. It's about how you respond to adversity and the commitment you show in your pursuit of success. Keep pushing forward, believing in yourself, and striving for the extraordinary. You have the power to create a future that reflects your deepest aspirations and dreams.

As we pressed forward in the season, our team managed to string together a few more victories, but then we encountered another formidable opponent, the Maple Grove Red Dragons. With a storied history and multiple State Championships under their belts over the past twenty years, the Red Dragons were a force to be reckoned with. We approached the game with confidence, or so we thought, only to find ourselves humbled. They relied on a roster filled with seasoned veterans and defeated us soundly, 28-14, on our home turf.

We faced one more loss that regular season, but fate granted us a rematch against the Red Dragons in the playoffs. This time, we would step onto their field, illuminated by the bright lights of Friday night. Despite being a young team, we were resolute in our commitment to compete at every level of the game, ready to prove ourselves. As a football coach, I can attest that this game ranks among the top five I've ever experienced. The intensity was palpable as we battled back and forth, trading plays, and matching their every inch. We fought valiantly, but when the final whistle blew, we fell short once again.

The bitter taste of that defeat lingered long after the game had ended. The Red Dragons moved forward in the playoffs, while our Wolfpack would have to retreat back to our den, reflecting on what went wrong. Yet, it was during this offseason that something profound began to shift within our players. They started to internalize a belief that they truly belonged, igniting a newfound commitment to Ty's system and their own development.

This experience taught us that every setback can be a springboard for personal and collective growth. While defeat can sting and leave scars, it is also fertile ground for cultivating resilience and determination. It is during these challenging times that we learn who we really are and what we're capable of achieving. Embracing the more difficult moments can ultimately strengthen our resolve and clarify our vision for the future.

As you pursue your own goals, remember that obstacles are often the catalysts for growth. Embrace the challenges that come your way, and use them as opportunities to build belief in yourself and your team, whatever that may look like in your life. Over time, as you face your own 'Red Dragons'—the formidable challenges that seek to deter you—let each experience mold you, and allow each loss to fuel your motivation for a comeback. Ultimately, it's about instilling a mindset that recognizes the value of hard work, dedication, and a belief in oneself. Know that you have the power to transform your journey into one of triumph, resilience, and enduring success. When you invest in your growth and align with those who uplift and inspire you, you'll unlock your potential to achieve greatness. So, dig deep, stay committed, and keep moving forward, for your most significant progress may lie just beyond the next challenge.

The 2018 season marked a pivotal moment for our coaching staff as we recognized our ability to compete with the best teams in our league. Throughout this journey, Ty Harper could have easily thrown in the towel and listened to those who suggested an alternative approach, but he remained steadfast in his vision and followed his plan. Ty was one of the first individuals I knew personally who truly embodied the principles of an Iron Life.

As summer transitioned into fall, our hard work began to pay off. We garnered attention statewide and found ourselves ranked among the Top 20 small schools. Instead of getting caught up in the hype, we focused on the fundamentals, each rep, each practice, and each game. Our ultimate test that season came against the formidable Red Dragons, a team we faced three times. It's never easy to devise a strategy against the same opponent repeatedly. In game two of the season, our team was ready.

We came out swinging, decisively beating the Red Dragons with a score of 55-20. The momentum was exhilarating. Fast forward to Week 6, and we faced them once again, this time at our home field. The Red Dragons underestimated us no longer. They entered the game with a renewed sense of resolve. It was a fierce battle, with both teams fighting for every down and striving for every score. Ultimately, we scraped by with a hard-fought 25-20 victory.

The final test of the year awaited in the playoffs, where we once again faced the Red Dragons, this time defeating them decisively with a score of 35-7. From there, we rolled through the rest of the playoffs and capped off our season with a triumphant 26-6 win in the State Championship. The wait and the hard work had been well worth it, and for Ty, this achievement was just the beginning of his illustrious coaching career. If you mention exceptional football coaches in our area, Ty Harper's name is a constant, and any conversation without him is simply incomplete.

The following year, he went on to win another State Championship, suffering only one loss throughout the season. Since that victorious 2018 season, Ty has compiled an impressive overall record of 43 wins to 8 losses, a remarkable turnaround from where we started. Recently, I had the opportunity to sit down with my longtime friend and mentor and ask him a few questions about patience and perseverance in the face of challenges. His insights reminded me that true success often requires time, dedication, and an unwavering belief in oneself. Here's what he had to say...

Q. Is there a secret to improving your quality of patience when it comes to the pursuit of a dream or a goal?

Ty: "I'm not sure if there is really a secret to improving one's patience, but I always drew inspiration from the most successful figures in sports. It's incredibly rare for an athlete or coach, (or business person or musician), to achieve immediate success. Many of the most successful people failed and patiently worked at their craft, refusing to give up until their goal was met or exceeded. No one wanted Tom Brady. He was the 199th pick in the 6th round of the 2000 NFL Draft. Six quarterbacks were taken ahead of him. He didn't start a single game during his rookie season.

It took Michael Jordan seven years to win a championship as a professional basketball player.

I saw Nick Saban speak at a football clinic in Pittsburgh in 2017, and he told an amazing story. During his first season at Alabama in 2007, they lost at home to Louisiana-Monroe (one of the greatest upsets in the history of college football). After the game, Saban entered a Tuscaloosa gas station, and when he walked up to the counter to pay, the attendant didn't recognize him. The guy asked if he (Saban) had watched the game, and proceeded to tell him that "Bama" would never win with Saban coaching the team.

Coach Saban smiled politely and said, "You might be right about that," paid, and exited the gas station.

The people that have accomplished the most have failed, some of them multiple times. That's something that always brought me comfort, as I was starting out as a head coach, especially when I failed. Great things don't usually happen, right away."

Q. What does patience mean to you?

Ty: "Patience is extremely underrated in accomplishing anything of real value. We live in a society where people young and old want instant results. People will say things like 'I worked really hard today. Why can't I see my abs, yet?'

It's the same thing with building a business or a competitive sports team. Change doesn't happen overnight, especially when you're trying to fix a culture of failure, or build a culture from scratch. I think if you talked to 100 successful people in various fields, they would all tell you that patience in the face of doubt was one of the most critical pieces to achieving success. It's hard to be patient when you know what you want your program (or business, or whatever) to look like, and it's just not there yet.

People are vocal when they're dissatisfied with the job that you're doing, especially in athletics. It's really frustrating to be yelled at, told that you don't know what you're doing, etc. I think that's the difference between people that accomplish really incredible things, and those that don't. It's a lot easier to throw your hands up and quit in the face of adversity than it is to be patient, work as hard as you can with no one watching, and persevere through the tough times. I don't have any data on this, but I'd be willing to bet that most really successful people had to battle through other people's doubt to achieve their ambitions."

Ty Harper is an exceptionally talented individual who excels in various areas of life, and he is someone I deeply aspire to emulate. He is a humble coach, driven by a genuine desire to win football games while guiding his players in a positive direction.

I vividly recall several instances following tough losses where, rather than dwelling on the disappointment of being behind on the scoreboard, Ty approached each postgame speech with a focus on positivity and growth. In those critical moments, whether we won or lost, he had a remarkable ability to extract valuable lessons and apply them to the broader journey of personal development for each young adult in the team. He often reminded us that a person's true character is not defined by their victories but rather revealed in how they handle setbacks and losses.

This profound insight has always resonated with me,

shaping my own philosophy and something I actively preach and embody in my life today. Ty, I want to express my heartfelt gratitude for the integral role you've played in shaping me into the man and the coach I am today. Your lessons have been invaluable, and they will forever influence how I approach challenges both on and off the field. Thank you for your unwavering support and for inspiring me to recognize the importance of resilience, character, and continuous growth in the journey of life. Your impact reaches far beyond the football field, and I am grateful for everything you have taught me.

IRONMAN

When I registered for the Maryland Ironman, I set my sights on a goal that was nearly eleven months away. At that distance from my destination, it's challenging to grasp the sheer volume of work and the intricacies of the process ahead. Even more elusive is understanding how all that effort will ultimately pay off.

In today's fast-paced society, we are often conditioned to believe that significant goals can be achieved in minimal time. This notion is perpetuated frequently through movies and television shows, leading to what I refer to as the "montage falsehood."

One of my favorite examples of this phenomenon can be vividly seen in the iconic film *Rocky IV*. In the story, Rocky Balboa has just suffered a devastating loss with the death of his best friend, Apollo Creed, at the hands of the formidable boxer, Ivan Drago. At that point, Rocky is far from being in fighting condition, yet he makes an unwavering commitment to travel to Russia on Christmas Day to face the "Siberian Express."

As the film builds towards the climactic fight, we witness a montage of Rocky's training regimen. The sequence includes scenes of him braving the harsh elements, carrying heavy logs through snowdrifts, lifting trailers filled with people, performing sit-ups from the second floor of an old barn illuminated by flickering firelight, and eventually climbing to the top of a snowy mountain. This entire training montage lasts about four minutes, creating a compelling cinematic experience. Notwithstanding, these highlight reels can distort our understanding of reality, instilling false hope that we can achieve monumental goals in a matter of days or weeks.

The truth is that real growth and development, the strengthening of the essential areas in our lives, requires time, dedication, and consistent effort. We must recognize that the element of time plays a critical role in shaping our journeys. Achieving meaningful outcomes is not merely about quick fixes or spurts of intense training. It's about cultivating endurance and fortitude as we navigate the myriad challenges we may encounter along the way. The journey to remarkable achievements, whether it's completing an Ironman, earning a degree, or pursuing any of life's ambitions, requires a sustained commitment to the process.

Embrace the time that it takes to progress. Every moment spent working towards your goal builds a foundation for future success. Understand that every step you take, no matter how small, is significant. Be patient with yourself and stay focused on the journey, for it is within this perseverance that you will discover the strength to push through adversity, rise up after setbacks, and ultimately reach the heights you aspire to achieve. So, as you embark on your quests, remember that while the road may seem long, each step forward brings you closer to your destination. Let go of the illusion of instant transformation and commit to the process of growth.

With countless hours of training ahead of me, the event felt like it was an eternity away. I often found myself wishing for the day to arrive already, imagining the moment I could swim 2.4 miles, bike 112 miles, and run 26.2 miles, all at once. I dreamt of snapping my fingers or completing a quick four-minute medley of exercises, just like Rocky Balboa preparing for his epic showdown against Ivan Drago in the Russian tundra. If only it were that simple!

Despite my mental desire to cut a few corners and skip some crucial phases of training, the reality was that I was far from being physically prepared for such an incredible undertaking. Saturday morning, August 5th, emerged as one of the toughest physical tests I had ever faced. I had scheduled a two-hour and thirty-minute run—a daunting task made even more challenging by the oppressive humidity of the day.

In a moment of poor judgment, I decided to embark on this long run on minimal fuel. Sure, I had consumed a substantial meal the night before, but I neglected the basics of hydration and proper nourishment when I woke up. As I left my house, I initially felt fantastic. My legs felt light, and I was clear-headed and focused. I'd settled into a comfortable rhythm, each step feeling as effortless as if my feet were floating on air. Everything seemed to be on track. The Barmore front was holding strong.

This sense of euphoria quickly vanished when I reached the ninth mile. Suddenly, it felt as if time had slowed down, and I was blindsided without warning. The exhaustion struck me like a freight train. It was as if I had just charged head-first into a brick wall, with the impact analogous to being tackled by Matt

Milano, the formidable linebacker of the Buffalo Bills during a heated Monday Night Football game.

The change was drastic and disorienting, and I realized just how unprepared I was for the physical demands of my goal. This experience served as a vivid reminder of the importance of proper preparation and self-care along the journey toward any goal. Success isn't just about the mental game. It's heavily influenced by how well you fuel and care for your body. While ambition drives us to tackle enormous challenges, neglecting what we need in order to perform can lead to unexpected setbacks and dismal outcomes.

As I regrouped mentally in those challenging moments, I learned that the journey of pursuing grand ambitions is not linear. It is filled with ups and downs, and it requires the willingness to adapt, recalibrate, and push through discomfort, both physically and mentally. In retrospect, each challenge we encounter is an opportunity for growth and learning. The key is to be mindful of how we treat ourselves throughout this journey.

Take the time to nourish your body and mind properly. Stay hydrated, plan for the long haul, and remember that achieving significant goals requires foundational work and preparation. Your own journey may not mirror mine, but the lessons remain universally applicable. Whether you're training for an Ironman, pursuing a new career, or striving for personal growth, the philosophy is the same: Prepare well, stay committed, and embrace both the highs and lows along the way. By doing so, you'll not only be ready to overcome challenges but also discover the true joy in the journey itself.

As I pushed through my run, I found myself just shy of the halfway point, anxiously awaiting the moment when my tracker would indicate that it was time to turn around. To keep my spirits up, I began identifying visible landmarks, like a distant telephone pole or a nearby mailbox, and I mentally told myself that if I could just reach those markers, I would soon arrive at the halfway mark. With each passing landmark, my steps felt increasingly heavier, yet I pressed on.

Despite my best efforts, I thought my Nike Run App failed to alert me when I had reached the halfway point. At one moment, I became convinced it had stopped tracking my progress altogether. Frustrated and fatigued, I paused briefly to check my device and confirm whether it was still functioning.

To my dismay, I realized my app was working just fine. I still had quite a distance to cover. This realization was demoralizing. With each step I took on the blistering asphalt, I felt like I was moving farther away from home and closer to my limits. My legs grew heavier with every passing moment, and my body was drenched in sweat, leading me to question my abilities and commitment to this challenge. From the waist down, I felt as if I were burning with fatigue, and to make matters worse, my once-saturated shirt began to dry, a clear indicator that dehydration was approaching.

As I jogged, I noticed small puddles of water at the edge of the road, remnants of rain that had clearly evaporated under the relentless sun. Each time I ran past one, an impulsive thought crossed my mind: 'What's the worst that could happen if I took a quick sip from one of those puddles?' Thankfully, I fought against that urge.

While I had made some questionable choices in my early twenties, I knew I was not about to cross the line into desperation by drinking from the roadside. As I continued onward, my stomach began to rumble, signaling that my fuel levels were plummeting along with my energy. Each step took me further away from the comfort of home, and the only thoughts racing through my mind were fixated on food and hydration.

In that feeling of uncertainty and rising anxiety, I understood that every great achievement comes with its share of discomfort and testing moments. This experience served as both a reminder and a lesson. The journey toward your goals is rarely smooth. It is often punctuated with struggles that can challenge your resolve. While it might seem easy to succumb to exhaustion or desperation in difficult moments, it is vital to trust your training and preparation. Instead of allowing negative thoughts to spiral, focus on finding solutions and pushing through the discomfort.

Remember, as you navigate your own challenges, whether they be physical, emotional, or professional, the key is to maintain your focus and remind yourself of the bigger picture. Just as I learned to find motivation in the small victories, you too can draw strength from each milestone along your path. Acknowledge the discomfort, confront your fears, and keep moving forward. The finish line may seem distant now, but every struggle you endure is a stepping stone closer to your dreams. In moments where the temptation to give up becomes overwhelming, remind yourself of your purpose and the fulfillment that awaits you on the other side of this journey. Embrace each experience, understand that it is all part of the process, and allow your determination to carry you through. You hold the power to transform hardships into profound lessons, emerging stronger, wiser, and more resilient than before. So, lace up those running shoes, push through the pain, and let the pursuit of your goals ignite the fire within you!

I typically pride myself on being a sub-nine-minute mile runner, comfortably maintaining a pace somewhere between eight and nine minutes per mile. With that said, on this particular day, I found myself creeping dangerously close to a ten-minute mile. Just when I thought my struggle would never end, Boom! My run tracker finally provided some encouraging news. I had reached the halfway point, and it was time to turn around.

While relief washed over me at the thought of heading back, I quickly remembered that I still had roughly eight more miles to cover. Each footfall seemed heavier than the last as I pushed myself forward, struggling to muster the energy to lift one foot after another. Under the relentless sun, my mind raced with excuses, desperately trying to convince me that I could give in to the discomfort. 'Just one more step,' I urged myself, repeating the mantra over and over again.

I couldn't help but think about my two-year-old son and how impressionable he is at this age. What would he think of his father if I quit now? What about my family, my students, my athletes, and my clients. How would they perceive my decision to throw in the towel? These thoughts kept me going, fueling my resolve to press on despite my growing fears of failing to meet the expectations I had set for myself.

At that moment, self-doubt began to creep into my mind, and I wondered if I had digressed in my training. With just over a month remaining until the Ironman, was I truly sliding backward? How was this possible? Why was I feeling this way?

But as those questions swirled in my head, I reminded myself of one vital truth. It didn't matter why or how I felt, the only choice was to keep going. The agony coursing through my feet, ankles, knees, and hips was no small feat to endure. As I continued my run, I reached a crucial juncture where I had two options. I could take a left turn that would allow me to cut approximately ten minutes off my run, or I could continue straight and stay true to my original plan.

In that exact moment of decision, the skeptical voice of negativity screamed at me to turn left and take the shortcut. 'Just go home!' it urged, trying to seduce me into abandoning my goal. But I knew better. I had to fight back against that voice. Finally, I found the strength within myself to win that critical mental battle. I pressed on, deciding not only to run straight but also to embrace the discomfort that accompanied my choice.

This decision was not merely about the physical task at hand, it was a testament to my commitment to ongoing growth and perseverance. Each time we encounter a moment of hesitation, we are given the opportunity to empower ourselves. It's in these testing moments that we discover our true capabilities and grow as individuals.

As you pursue your own goals, remember that feeling overwhelmed is normal, and the desire to cut corners may tempt you. Stand strong against that inner critic. Every time you resist the easier path, you reinforce your resilience and commitment to your growth. As you travel along your journey, take note of those pivotal moments that challenge you. Acknowledge that pushing through discomfort and confronting your doubts will ultimately lead to greater strength and achievement. Choose to embrace the struggle, remain steadfast in your intentions, and keep moving forward one step at a time, for it is through these moments of courage that you will forge the path to your ultimate success.

I refused to engage in a debate with the voice inside my head that urged me to take the easy way out. As I distanced myself from that tempting left turn, my mental state began to wage a war against my resolve. The thought lurked in the background, whispering that I could easily turn back and shave off a considerable amount of time from my effort. Yet, as each agonizing step brought me further away from that tempting shortcut, it became clear to me that I would never allow myself to live with regret. From that moment forward, taking the easy route would no longer be an option in my life. As I continued on my journey, what felt like an hour had actually only been about twenty minutes, but the relentless fight to maintain my focus felt monumental. I rounded the final corner of my run, and a wave of pure joy washed over me.

Typically, I can push through the pain and fatigue to sprint the last stretch of any run, but this time was an exception to my usual resilience. I found myself devoid of energy, feeling as if I had nothing left in the tank. I was utterly depleted, physically drained and mentally defeated. I wondered how I would ever recover from this grueling experience. Only time would reveal the answer. As I finally reached my home, I staggered inside, reaching for a refreshing orange Gatorade to replenish my depleted body. I sank down to the floor, utterly spent, questioning how I would ever muster the strength to get back on my feet.

It's essential to recognize that we all face moments of profound challenge, where our mental fortitude is tested and our commitment is questioned. It is during these taxing experiences that we have the opportunity to learn about our true strength and resilience. We may encounter feelings of exhaustion and defeat, but it's how we respond to those feelings that will ultimately define our journey.

In those moments of vulnerability, it's crucial to remind

yourself of the progress you've made and the goals you still wish to achieve. Although you might feel like you're at your last gasps of energy, it's essential to keep pushing forward. Each setback can be a powerful teacher if you allow it to be. The key is to honor your experience, take the time you need to recover, and then recommit to rising again.

As you navigate the challenges in your own life, remember to listen to that inner voice urging you to push through, even when every fiber of your being wants to give up. Embrace the discomfort and recognize that it is part of the growth process. Like me, you may find yourself on the ground, exhausted and questioning your perseverance, but take heart. The moment you rise again is where the true magic happens.

The next time life throws a challenge your way, resist the urge to take the easy path. Stand firm in your commitment to your goals, and give yourself permission to feel the discomfort, knowing it is simply a stepping stone toward a brighter, more fulfilling future. After all, it's in those moments of struggle that we discover our ability to bounce back, stronger and more determined than ever. Keep moving forward, because the best is yet to come!

When faced with a sudden shift in momentum, especially during days filled with distress and discomfort, it's all too easy to become your own worst enemy. In these critical moments, it is essential to adhere to your plan and combat any impatience that may arise. To navigate these challenging times, I rely on my "**WINN Method**" as a powerful reminder that even when I stumble, I have not truly failed.

Failure is seldom a permanent condition unless you allow it to define you. It's crucial to remember that each setback can serve as a valuable lesson rather than an endpoint. By maintaining a mindset focused on growth and resilience, you can transform what seems like a failure into an opportunity for progress. Embrace the journey, and remember that perseverance in the face of adversity is the true hallmark of success.

Where were you? It's important to take a moment to recognize your current situation, to really assess where you stand in relation to your goals and aspirations. Understanding your present circumstances is the first crucial step on the path to transformation.

By acknowledging where you are, you pave the way for identifying what it will take to bridge the gap between your current state and the destination you wish to reach. Reflecting on your current position allows you to gain clarity about the obstacles you may face and the steps you need to take to overcome them. Are there skills you need to develop? Habits that require adjustment? Support systems that are missing?

By answering these questions, you can create a roadmap that guides your journey toward your desired goals. Setting clear and actionable objectives will enable you to chart a course back to where you want to be. It's not just about recognizing the distance to your goals. It's about acknowledging the effort and preparation required to close that gap. As you embark on this journey, remember that self-awareness is a cornerstone of personal development. Embrace this opportunity for introspection and honest evaluation. Invest the time and effort to understand not just where you are now, but also the commitment it will take to make the necessary changes for the future.

By doing so, you set yourself up for success and develop a proactive mindset that ensures you are always moving in the right direction, towards the life you envision and deserve. So, ask yourself: Where am I? And more importantly, What steps will I take to move forward? Your journey of self-discovery and growth begins with these simple yet powerful questions. Embrace the process, and take ownership of your path forward!

Incorporate your vision and bring it to life! It's vital to hold onto that vision, especially during your moments of struggle. After all, those challenging days of training often prove to be the most significant in your overall development. You might feel as if you have completely failed on such days, but I assure you, that is far from the truth. We all encounter off days, those times when everything seems to go awry. But it's crucial to remember that each of these moments holds significant value.

Use these experiences as powerful tools in your journey. When faced with adversity, whether it be feelings of oppression, setbacks, or mishaps, the focus should not be on dwelling in negativity. Instead, shift your perspective to extract meaningful lessons from these experiences. These lessons will help you rebound stronger the next time you find yourself in a similar situation.

This practice of reflection and learning is imperative for personal growth and the ongoing development of your 'Iron story'—the narrative of resilience and strength that you build throughout your life. Each struggle adds a chapter, contributing to the richness of your journey and shaping your character. Approach every setback as an opportunity to learn and grow, turning those experiences into stepping stones toward your ultimate vision. As you navigate your path, remind yourself that it's through these trials that the true essence of your strength is revealed.

Keep your vision alive, learn from your moments of struggle, and use them as fuel to propel you forward. Your Iron story is waiting to be written, one powerful chapter at a time!

Notice how your body and mind are feeling right now. What sensations are you experiencing, and why might your body feel this way? What thoughts are racing through your mind, and what could be contributing to those feelings? It's important to reflect on how well you prepared yourself for this significant training day or event. Did you approach the night before with intention, ensuring you set yourself up for success, or did you neglect to plan and, as a result, fail to give yourself the best chance to thrive?

In my own experience, there were days when I found myself unprepared, setting me up for a series of blunders. The weight of those mistakes lingered in my mind, playing psychological games with me for weeks on end. I was left grappling with self-doubt, questioning my capability to rebound and rise above the challenges. I realized this period of feeling overwhelmed played a crucial role in my training journey. I took full responsibility for my lack of preparation. I acknowledged that I hadn't equipped myself properly for what lay ahead, and it became abundantly clear that I needed to strengthen both my mind and body to pave a successful path as I moved forward. I could not allow my earlier missteps to become a hindrance to the person I aspired to become over the following months.

Recognizing and owning your feelings is a critical aspect of personal growth. When our bodies and minds communicate discomfort or uncertainty, they are inviting us to examine our choices and adjust our approaches. This self-awareness leads to valuable insights that can significantly enhance our performance and resilience. Moving forward, commit to embracing a holistic approach to preparation—mind, body, and spirit.

Understand that the effort you put in before the big day is just as important as the day itself. Foster healthy habits, ensure proper sleep, nutrition, and mental clarity, and every aspect of your preparation will contribute to your overall success. The challenges you face are not merely obstacles. They are lessons that inform your growth and development. Transform those moments of doubt into opportunities for strengthening resolve. No matter how far you feel from your goals, remember that each experience, whether successful or not, adds valuable knowledge to your toolkit.

As you navigate your journey, don't allow temporary setbacks to define your self-worth or your potential. Instead, view them as essential components of your story, a story filled with resilience, determination, and an unyielding will to become the best version of yourself. Embrace the responsibility for your preparation, reflect on your experiences, refine your approach, and take actionable steps to ensure you're ready for whatever challenges lie ahead.

Your destiny is a product of your choices, and by approaching every aspect of your path with intention, you embrace the transformative journey toward achieving your goals. You have the power within you to overcome. Now is your time to prepare and succeed!

No matter the circumstances, the key is to proceed. Keep moving forward. It's a requisite to remind yourself that even if you didn't have your best day, perhaps you even had your worst day, you must continue onward. From this point forward, be intentional and deliberate in both your mental strength and the actions you take.

All smiles transitioning from my swim into the bike in Cambridge, Maryland.
Barmore Photo Collection

Remember, you are here for a reason, and you have every

right to be on this journey. You belong. While this transitional period may feel like a minor stroke in the grand scheme of your life's masterpiece, it is unequivocally important. Each moment you encounter is an opportunity to proceed and execute your plans, no matter the cost. Understand that storms will inevitably roll in, but like all things, they will eventually pass if you're patient and give them time. Take control of your situation and shoulder the responsibility of manifesting the accomplishments you committed to achieving.

When the following week rolled around, I was all systems go. My training plan called for a ten-minute longer run than the previous week, and if you think I wasn't over prepared, then you're not quite grasping my dedication. The night before, I treated myself to a celebratory meal that had become a pre-training ritual: a hearty pasta dish paired with a fresh salad and plenty of garlic bread, all washed down with a chilled IPA.

My go-to meals typically consist of Chicken Parmesan with noodles or Eggplant Parmesan accompanied by a spinach salad loaded with nuts and a deliciously oily dressing. On the side, I indulged in three to six slices of garlic bread, ensuring I was well-fueled and ready to tackle the day ahead. This may seem like a hefty meal, but through several years of trial and error, I have honed in on what works best for me. Come morning, when my alarm buzzed at 3:37 AM, two hours before my demanding training session, I ensured that I began my day with a bagel spread with peanut butter.

More food equals more fuel, but it's crucial to listen to your body and fuel appropriately for action, rather than simply filling your stomach. Keep in mind that everyone's needs are unique. I made sure to stay properly hydrated, consuming two small water bottles along with a Gatorade to replenish my electrolytes. For this particular day on the road, I also packed a few Huma Gels for a quick energy boost. While some prefer Gu or Gatorade gels, I have always been fond of Huma Chocolate gels. They're delicious and reminiscent of pudding, providing a much-needed lift when I start to feel weighed down.

This time, I didn't just survive my run, I thrived. I was smiling, enjoying every step of the journey. As I cycled my usual miles around Chautauqua Lake, I cleverly weaved in and out of side streets to meet my training distance, eventually hitting the back roads of a nearby small town for my run. I felt invigorated as I blazed through roads surrounded by picturesque cornfields and sprawling cow pastures. Despite the warmth of the summer day, I kept myself cool, both physically and mentally. My focus and determination were at their peak, and I was completely in my "A-Game."

To my amazement, I managed to shave off over twenty seconds per mile—yes, per mile! That additional time allowed me to cover nearly two miles further than I had expected. The secret? It's the WINN Approach, a system that emphasizes the importance of capitalizing on every training day as integral to your overarching masterpiece.

The day before leaving for Cambridge, Maryland. My sister Kari was with me several steps of the way.
Barmore Photo Collection

Never allow the clouds of a single bad day to obscure the brilliance of the sun that lies ahead. Remember, the storms of life will indeed pass, revealing brighter days on the horizon. Practice patience and perseverance, for you are in control of your journey. Embrace the challenges you face, enjoy the process, and know that every stride you take brings you closer to your dreams. Celebrate the progress, no matter how small, and continue to push forward. You possess the strength within you to achieve extraordinary things, so keep moving, keep believing, and keep striving for greatness!

CHAPTER 8

P - P

PERSISTENCY

Failure should never be perceived as a negative experience. Instead, it should be embraced as a foundational stepping stone on the journey to personal growth and achievement. Each misstep or setback presents a valuable lesson that when acknowledged and understood, can significantly enhance our knowledge and development.

Consider the legendary inventor Thomas Edison, who famously encountered countless failures in his quest to create the standard light bulb. When questioned about his many unsuccessful attempts, he offered a perspective that is both inspiring and illuminating: "I have not failed. I've just found 10,000 ways that don't work."

This statement encapsulates the essence of persistence and resilience. The ability to persevere in the face of adversity is what ultimately opens the door to tremendous rewards and breakthroughs in life. Each setback we encounter should not be labeled as a failure, rather, it should be recognized as an important opportunity to recalibrate our approach and evolve in our journey toward success.

Think of life as a vast and intricate jigsaw puzzle. Each piece represents an experience, a lesson learned, or a challenge faced. If you throw in the towel and concede defeat before you have made a relentless effort to piece together your unique puzzle, you will never reveal the beautiful final picture that is your life. Embracing the complexities of this puzzle means remaining committed to seeing how all the pieces fit together, regardless of how confusing or frustrating the process may seem.

In times of struggle, remind yourself that every single experience, whether positive or negative, contributes to your development. It helps you build resilience and fortitude necessary to navigate the tougher moments ahead. Each time you fall short of your goals, ask yourself: What can I learn from this? How can this experience refine me and prepare me for the next challenge? Do not fear failure. Embrace it, learn from it, and actually utilize its lessons to propel you forward. The road to achievement is rarely straight and it often winds its way through challenges that will test your resolve and character. By approaching these challenges with a mindset rooted in learning and growth, you'll transform each perceived setback into a powerful catalyst for future success.

Understand that persistence in the face of failure is not just an admirable trait, it is essential for creating the life you envision. So, face your fears head-on, refuse to be discouraged, and remain committed to your journey. Remember, the only true failure is in not trying at all. Make every attempt count, and let each experience shape you into the best version of yourself. With this attitude and approach, you're bound to discover that with every setback comes the incredible opportunity to rise again, stronger and wiser than before. Keep piecing together your jigsaw puzzle, one bold move at a time, and watch as the masterpiece of your life unfolds in glorious detail.

LIFE

I still vividly remember my experience in fourth grade during our class production of *The Polar Express*. Though I didn't land a leading role, my character had multiple lines that I was expected to deliver in front of what felt like hundreds of strangers. At that age, the thought of public speaking filled me with an overwhelming sense of anxiety. It's a fear many kids face as they grapple with the idea of being watched. I struggled with a deep-seated fear of performance, feeling my heart race as I stumbled through my words, mumbled incoherently, and stuttered as I tried to speak. I was a far cry from the confident elf I needed to portray.

During our very first rehearsal, with the spotlight shining brightly on me, I delivered half of my lines filled with uncertainty. I honestly wasn't sure if anyone could even comprehend what I was trying to say. The embarrassment washed over me, and I felt completely broken inside. The weight of judgment from everyone in that rehearsal room felt suffocating, and the desire to give up surged within me, accompanied by a temptation to hide from the world.

My teacher, sensing my struggle, even offered me the option to step away from the role. As I sat on the bench, grappling with my internal battle, the door swung open and Mrs. Johnson entered the room. This pivotal moment in my young life is a testament to the challenges we all face when stepping outside our comfort zones. It wasn't just about memorizing lines or performing. It was about wrestling with my fears and learning to confront them head-on.

Much like preparing for a triathlon, this experience taught me vital lessons about courage, resilience, and the power of pushing beyond perceived limitations. Each time you take on a challenge, be it public speaking, competing in a triathlon, or any significant endeavor, you are venturing into the unknown. And just as I had to navigate my anxiety during that play, you too will face hurdles that test your determination and will.

Preparation entails more than just training your body physically. It involves silencing that internal voice of doubt, acknowledging your fears, and transforming them into motivation. When you enter that water, hop on the bike, or take that first step on the run, it's about pushing through discomfort and embracing every moment of the journey.

As I reflect on my experience in *The Polar Express*, I realize that the struggle to overcome the fear of performance was instrumental in shaping my character. It was a reminder that it's okay to be vulnerable and that these growth opportunities, regardless of how intimidating they may be, can lead to profound personal transformations.

As you prepare for your own unique challenges, whether they be in triathlon training or any other aspects of life, remember that it's normal to feel fear and anxiety. Embrace those feelings, allow them to guide you, but don't let them deter you. Just as I sought out support from my teacher, reach out to those who motivate you, and lean on your support system to bolster your confidence.

When the spotlight is on you, whether in a classroom, on a racecourse, or in life, hold your head high and push forward. Every accomplishment begins with the courage to step onto the stage and face your fears. Celebrate your progress, and remember that it's the journey of growth that genuinely defines your success. Trust in yourself, seize the opportunity, and approach each new challenge with the unwavering determination to prevail. Your masterpiece awaits, and each step you take brings you closer to realizing it!

Mrs. Johnson approached me with a kindness and gentleness that immediately put me at ease. Placing her hand on my back, she asked me point-blank whether I wanted to keep the role I had been assigned or pass it along to a friend. As a child, I struggled to grasp the concept of quitting. It's a trait that often develops as we grow older and encounter disappointment or denial of our desires. I longed to be part of the production alongside my friends, so I mustered all my resolve and confidently told her that I would keep my role, promising myself that I would do better next time.

With determination, I took the rehearsal pamphlet home and recited my lines repeatedly. I practiced in front of the mirror, rehearsed for my mother, performed for my siblings, and even showcased my lines to my friends. I was resolved not to let this opportunity slip away. In my heart, I firmly believe that life is all about second chances, and I was ready to seize mine. The following week, we returned for another rehearsal. I was up once more, filled with an exhilarating combination of excitement and anxiety.

As I stepped into the center of the stage, confidence radiated from every pore in my body. In that moment, I felt as if I were auditioning for a role in a film like *Good Will Hunting*, convinced I could land the part. But then, as soon as they called out "Action," everything changed.

In an instant, my confidence evaporated. Anxiety surged

through me as I felt my blood pressure rise and my heart begin to race. It felt as if I were about to vomit from sheer nervousness. Why was I reacting this way? After all, I had practiced diligently, putting in the effort to master my lines, yet I still fell short of delivering the performance I had envisioned.

At this critical juncture, I realized there are always two options when faced with moments of despair and self-doubt. You can either allow the fear to take over, letting it dictate your actions and define your experience, or you can choose to confront the challenge head-on, using it as a powerful opportunity for growth.

This experience mirrors the journey of completing an Ironman Triathlon so much. Just like standing on that stage, you will face moments when anxiety and fear threaten to derail your progress. Despite the emotion and feeling, it's important to remember that each challenge is an opportunity to push beyond your perceived limits. Embrace your discomfort and recognize that it's in these intense moments that you truly discover who you are and what you're capable of achieving. Similar to my Ironman, every stroke in the water, each mile on the bike, and every step of the run can feel monumental, especially when facing the elements or grappling with fatigue. But when you encounter these challenges, ask yourself: Will I let the fear win, or will I rise to the occasion and show up for myself?

Deciding to confront your fears rather than succumb to them is where the magic happens. It's in those moments of anxiety that you have the chance to forge resilience and character. Just like I had to remind myself before those rehearsals, you must continually affirm your commitment to your goals and embrace the journey with all its ups and downs.

Always remember, you are capable of far more than you realize. When the pressure mounts and the nerves set in, dig deep and find the courage to push through. Ultimately, it is not about perfection. It's about persistence and the unwavering belief that you can tackle any challenge before you.

With each moment you engage with truthfully and persistently, you sculpt a stronger version of yourself. So, approach your own challenges, whether they be in training or in life, with this mindset, and watch as you unlock the extraordinary potential that lies within you. We stand at a crucial crossroads in our lives. The choice between giving up and forever wondering "what if," or persisting and continuing to strive toward our goals.

That young boy from my past knew there was only one option: stay persistent and keep practicing. Growing up, I often heard the saying that "practice makes perfect," and at the time, I wholeheartedly believed it. The motivational speaker Les Brown offered a different perspective, one that resonated with me even more deeply. He stated, "Practice makes improvement," and he was absolutely right.

Each day, I made a conscious effort to improve, honing my skills until I felt sharp enough to deliver a strong performance. At that pivotal moment in my life, even if it was just a fourth-grade crossroads, I made a commitment to myself. I would rather face the anguish of failure than live in the shadow of regret, perpetually questioning what could have been. I refused to succumb to the temptation of quitting. That very night, I gathered my family in the living room, determined to put on a show. I rehearsed my lines over and over, not just once but again and again, night after night, until I felt I was beyond prepared.

When the following week arrived, I walked onto the stage

radiating poise and courage. This was my moment, and I wasn't about to let it slip away. I delivered my lines with such conviction that I felt as though I were standing on the bright lights of Broadway. And just like that, I did it! After stepping off the stage, I practically sprinted to the dressing room, overflowing with joy and excitement. The sheer exhilaration I felt from overcoming failure after failure culminated in this rewarding moment. Oftentimes, our greatest accomplishments serve as poignant reminders of the struggles and shortcomings we have endured. It's not unusual to see an athlete overcome with emotion after winning a championship as they are often reflecting on the many times they believed they were prepared, only to fall short.

Each of those moments, while painful, was transformed into fuel. Ammunition that propelled them toward achieving their hard-won success. So, as you navigate your own journeys and face the inevitable defeats, remember this: Recite your actions, recommit to your goals, and relentlessly pursue improvement until you achieve success. Nothing worthwhile in life is simply handed to you. You have to earn it one day at a time. Whether through one rehearsal at a time or consistent effort in your daily endeavors, stay committed to becoming the person you aspire to be.

IRONMAN

The challenges I faced during my Ironman training were unlike anything I had ever encountered in any previous experience. When I signed up for this event, I didn't fully grasp what it would entail, but one thing I knew for certain was that the only element within my complete control was my actions. I quickly realized that I would have no influence over external factors like the weather.

There was a three-week stretch during my training where I saw little to no improvement in my times, physical strength, or overall performance. These periods in life can be pivotal, distinguishing those who ultimately find success from those who succumb to doubt and discouragement. I came to refer to this challenging phase as "the drought," a time when it felt like every conceivable obstacle was being thrown my way.

One particularly grueling experience occurred on a Saturday training day that required me to complete a four-hour bike ride followed by an hour and a half run. As I reached the third hour of the bike ride, I was suddenly enveloped by a torrential downpour, a Western New York monsoon that tested my resilience like never before. Each drop of rain seemed to mock me, as if Mother Nature herself were taunting me to quit and return home. But instead of surrendering to the storm, I gritted my teeth and kept pedaling, reminding myself that with every turn of the pedal, I was inching closer to home. Each rotation took me further down the path toward achieving my goal of becoming an Ironman. And so, pedal after pedal, I pushed through the downpour until I finally reached my destination, soaked but triumphant.

During these moments of extreme difficulty that threaten to instill self-doubt, it's crucial to dig deep within yourself and find the reservoir of strength you didn't know you had. These are the times that test our endurance and resolve, and they are essential to our growth. It can be all too simple to lie down and succumb to the desire to make excuses for why things aren't working out. Anyhow, the imperative lesson is to seek a way forward instead of allowing yourself to be sidelined by setbacks. Embrace the discomfort, confront your challenges head-on, and tackle each obstacle with determination.

The resilience you build through navigating these hardships not only prepares you for future obstacles but also enhances your ability to achieve greatness. So next time you find yourself in a difficult situation, consider how you can adapt and push through. Transform your "drought" into an opportunity for growth, and recognize that true success is often found on the other side of adversity. By fueling your determination with persistence and courage, you can overcome anything and continue your journey toward the remarkable life you envision for yourself. Hold onto that inner strength—each challenge brings you one step closer to your dreams!

The following week, I found myself grappling with a persistent pain that nagged at me with each turn of the pedals during my bike ride. I woke up at 3:30 AM on a Saturday morning filled with confidence. I was ready to tackle the day. After enjoying a hearty meal the night before and a light breakfast to fuel my workout, I felt prepared to embark on a grueling four-plus hour training session. But as I set off on my bike, a mere mile into the ride, I began to feel a throbbing pain in my knee. With each pedal stroke, doubts flooded my mind. Could I really push through this discomfort? Would I be able to endure another three hours and fifty-five minutes of agony?

As the reality of the situation sank in, I knew I had to adjust my approach. I eased off on the intensity, but I made a conscious decision to keep moving forward, turning over the pedals despite the nagging pain. I initially feared that this setback would stall my progress, but to my surprise, I discovered a valuable lesson. I learned that I could establish preset limits and still extend my personal mental and physical boundaries. It was a pivotal realization that transformed my perspective on challenges.

As I continued pedaling, the agonizing sensation in my knee persisted, but I refused to let it defeat me. I remembered the comedic yet insightful strategy employed by Adam Sandler in the movie *Happy Gilmore*, where he channels his focus into a "happy place." I decided to implement this technique, using it as a tool to keep myself anchored in positivity and limit the negative thoughts that threatened to overtake my mind. Creating a positive mental image became my lifeline. I envisioned the sun shining brightly overhead and thought of my family, their support and encouragement lifting my spirits. I also reflected on the journey of self-discovery, considering the person I once was, the individual I had grown into, and the vision I held for the person I aspired to be.

This exercise in visualization not only distracted me from the discomfort in my knee but also rekindled my motivation to keep pushing forward. It reminded me that challenges are often temporary while the strength we cultivate in overcoming them can serve us for a lifetime.

Ironman Finisher
Barmore Photo Collection

As you face your own trials, whether they are physical challenges like a long bike ride or other hardships in life, remember that the mind is a powerful tool. It's crucial to harness that power to guide your thoughts away from negativity and toward positivity. By creating uplifting imagery in your mind, drawing on memories, aspirations, and moments of joy, you can fortify your courage and confidence. So, when the road gets tough or when you're confronted with discomfort, take a moment to visualize your happy place. Allow that mental image to fuel your determination, and remind yourself of your capacity to rise above challenges. Embrace the grind, lean on your mental strategies, and, just like me, you may find that you can extend your limits further than you ever believed possible.

Every step forward, no matter how small, is a testament to your inner strength and unwavering spirit. Keep pedaling, keep believing, and never underestimate the power of a positive mindset on your journey to greatness. Imagine experiencing the perfect day, one filled with nothing but pure joy and fulfillment. Envision the pursuit of a monumental achievement, but most importantly, picture yourself grasping the goal you've worked tirelessly for and desperately desired.

The adrenaline and excitement that accompanies such an accomplishment is immeasurable, and I began to realize that I was onto something. For me, my happy place is beautifully uncomplicated. It's a warm home, brimming with laughter from my family, the sweet aroma of a wood fire crackling in the background creating an inviting ambiance and setting a positive tone. In that space, there is nothing but love and connection with those I cherish most. As I indulged in these thoughts, I felt goosebumps and chills wash over me, transforming my discomfort and the pain in my knee into pure enthusiasm and energy.

This visualization was incredibly effective. Time began to slip away, and the miles seemed to float by with newfound ease. And then—BOOM! As the image became more vivid, I looked up and realized that I was approaching the last leg of my ride. The finish line was finally within reach! Reflecting on this experience, the number one lesson I took away was the immense power of positive imagery and self-belief. When you can envision yourself achieving remarkable things and channel that energy into the universe, you equip yourself with the tools to navigate even the roughest seas.

Moreover, I discovered a crucial principle that has shaped my journey. Success does not require perfection. Time and again, I've learned that choosing persistence over perfection is the key to overcoming obstacles. By cultivating intentional persistence, we can tackle even the most significant hurdles life presents to us. In embarking on your own journey, understand that both the highest peaks and the lowest valleys are essential. Each experience contributes to the tapestry of your resilience and growth. Both the triumphant moments and the challenging ones are equally important because they serve as the forge that shapes your character and tenacity.

The bike ride was the most memorable part of the entire Ironman event for me. It was the moment I could truly appreciate the 'final product' of all the hard work I had put in over the span of ten months. During the ride, I encountered eagles, snakes, various rodents, and even some fish. I was able to share encouraging words with fellow athletes and take in my surroundings, smiling in amazement at what I was accomplishing. Out of the 112 miles, 110 were nearly seamless and surprisingly enjoyable. However, in the final two miles, that nagging knee pain I had experienced weeks prior began to resurface. 'Happy place! Get to your happy place,' I reminded myself repeatedly.

Two miles turned into one, and before I knew it, I could see the finish line ahead. How was I already two-thirds of the way through this event? Ten months of hard work culminated in dismounting from my bike, entering the transition area, and mentally and physically preparing for the full marathon that lay ahead.

Never allow either extreme, whether high or low, to dictate your subsequent actions. In your darkest moments or in times of brilliance, remember that nothing is ever guaranteed. But if you maintain a foundation of belief and commit to consistent effort over time, you will inevitably rise from the valleys and find a way to remain atop the peaks. So, as you navigate your journey, fill your mind with positive imagery, uphold your determination, and embrace the power of persistence. By doing so, you will empower yourself to not only overcome the challenges in your path but to truly thrive in the wake of life's unpredictability. With each step forward, you're one step closer to crafting the amazing life you envision—one filled with joy, achievement, and a sense of purpose that comes from pursuing your passions with relentless dedication. Remember, it's not about being perfect. It's about staying committed to the process, believing in yourself, and pushing through the storms of life with gritty resolve. Your remarkable journey starts now, so take that step forward with unwavering courage!

REFLECTION

1. What is your Personal WINN?

W

(Where did you start?)

_____

_____

_____

_____

I

(Include your vision. What is it that you want to achieve?)

_____

_____

_____

_____

N

(Notice how your body/mind are feeling. Is your body/mind gaining strength?)

_____

_____

_____

_____

_____

N

(No matter what, proceed. We all have test days, how did you break through?)

_____

_____

_____

_____

Part 3

REPEAT

CHAPTER 9

THE CHECKERED FLAG

When you successfully complete a task that you've set out to achieve, you are not just checking an item off your to-do list, you are fortifying your confidence and strengthening your sense of self. With every accomplishment, you forge your inner strength, transforming it into something akin to iron, solid and unwavering right before your eyes. Each victory, no matter how small, adds layers to your self-assurance. You gain the understanding that with adequate preparation and consistent repetition, you can tackle any challenge with pride and resilience.

Experiencing a profound sense of achievement on a grand stage elevates your belief in yourself, affirming that you possess the ability to regroup and repeat the process as you further hone your skills toward that specific goal. This courage becomes an essential stimulant, propelling you to explore even larger ambitions and expand the boundaries of what you once considered impossible.

Within the framework of personal development, the phase of Prep-Rep-Repeat stands as the most crucial of the three stages. Many individuals find themselves wandering aimlessly at this juncture, which often leads to the loss of momentum and a drift away from their aspirations. Still, a select few will discover new light, harnessing that energy to pursue their dreams with renewed vigor.

It's common for us to work tirelessly, climbing the mountain toward substantial achievements and accolades. Yet, when we finally reach the summit, we sometimes allow ourselves to linger, looking around in awe for far too long. This can leave us feeling dazed, confused, and stagnant. While it's important to celebrate your achievements, lingering too long can prevent you from recognizing that the journey is far from over. Once you reach a significant milestone, don't forget to continue pushing yourself forward. Use the momentum you've built as fuel to set new challenges and goals. By doing so, you maintain the dynamic flow of progress rather than allowing it to stall.

Remember that the summit you've just conquered is merely a stepping stone. There are countless more peaks to scale. Moreover, embracing the mindset that each accomplishment is part of a larger continuum can profoundly alter your perspective on success. The moment you reach a goal, take a moment to acknowledge your hard work, absorb the joy of your achievement, and then ask yourself: What's next?

This reflective practice keeps you engaged and motivated, allowing you to build upon your previous success. In the end, take heart in knowing that each step you take is part of a powerful journey. By maintaining your determination and commitment to the Prep-Rep-Repeat process, you will find yourself continuously evolving and stretching the limits of what you can achieve. Keep moving forward, and let the lessons learned along the way illuminate your path toward even greater heights. The journey is ongoing, and it's time to embrace it fully.

Your next adventure awaits. Be ready to seize it with courage and tenacity! This is the most crucial moment to focus your energy, put the pedal to the metal, and ensure that you do not fall victim to the trap of over-celebration. While it's absolutely important to celebrate your victories—you've worked hard for them and should sincerely relish your achievements—it's equally vital to limit the timeframe of your triumphant praise. The longer you allow yourself to bask in glory, the deeper you settle into your previous start line, making it more challenging to move forward toward new goals. Take it from someone like Nick Saban, who expressed his frustration after winning the National Championship in 2013, stating, "that damn game cost me a week of recruiting."

True champions like Saban exemplify the importance of winning, but they also understand the necessity of maintaining a nimble mindset. They celebrate their successes briefly and then pivot to focus on what comes next. We've all encountered individuals who perpetually dwell on past achievements, hanging their identity on accomplishments from years gone by.

Think of that one football player who still recounts a legendary play against a rival team from fifteen years ago. They are usually the ones who cling tightly to the 18-year-old version of themselves, unable to evolve with the passage of time. It's perfectly acceptable to feel proud of your past accomplishments. That's what trophies, rings, and plaques are for. As those accolades accumulate dust, we must be mindful of the need to raise the bar and actively pursue what lies ahead. It's comforting to reflect on "what was," yet transitioning the narrative to "what could be" often presents a much more daunting challenge.

Now is the time to instill meaningful change and focus on your ongoing personal growth. While we often view the finish line, or the proverbial "light at the end of the tunnel" as the ultimate destination, it's critical to shift our perspective. A finish line should never merely be viewed as an endpoint. Instead, it ought to be treated as the starting point for your next grand exploration. Remind yourself that it's perfectly okay to applaud your efforts and to acknowledge the great things you've accomplished, yet don't allow yourself to become so entrenched in the past that you find it difficult to regain momentum. This isn't a debate where you weigh the merits of pursuing your next milestone. It's a definitive call to action. You must determine where you want to go and what you want to achieve with as much clarity and urgency as possible.

To aid you in the process of rebounding after reaching a milestone or goal, the Repeat Phase can be broken down into four essential steps. These steps will provide a roadmap for maintaining your momentum, ensuring you continue to push forward even after celebrating your achievements.

STEP 1: CURRENT SITUATION

Here you stand, having reached a significant milestone in your life. You've conquered an Ironman, crossed the finish line of a marathon, graced the stage at a physique competition, or perhaps you've just penned the final chapter of your novel. But now that you've accomplished this immense feat, you might be wondering, What's next?

The first step in this new chapter is to shift your mindset and prepare to embark on the journey once again. This moment is crucial. It's time to draw upon the discipline and fortitude you've cultivated over the past weeks, months, or even years.

Remember, you must become your own accountability partner. Sure, it might be easy to dodge responsibility by relying on your best friend, spouse, parents, or kids, but there is one person you can never escape—you.

Look into the mirror and confront yourself with honesty. Remind yourself that this is just the beginning. You are not going to settle for the status quo. Take control of your life, understanding that you have the ultimate authority over your next move.

This lifestyle isn't just about "Prep-Rep-Try Something New." It's about Prep-Rep-Repeat—a continuous cycle of commitment and achievement. To illustrate this process, consider the analogy of your quest for "Emerald City."

The initial step toward your destination involves pushing through a dense forest filled with challenges. The path ahead may be obscured by thick brush, overgrown trees, and a lack of a clear route. Every day presents an opportunity to carve a way through the undergrowth, to establish a pathway through the chaos.

As you persist in your efforts, you will notice the beginnings of a trail, evidence of your relentless determination. With every attempt, you're steadily shaping a path that others might follow. Eventually, after a series of arduous efforts, you will break through the forest and find yourself on the famed yellow brick road. But don't be fooled as this is not the end of your journey. This is where the adventure really begins.

Just because you've reached this significant milestone doesn't mean the challenges ahead will cease. In fact, it's in this space of achievement that new opportunities and goals will present themselves, calling for just as much dedication and strength as the ones you've already conquered. As you navigate this next leg of your journey, remain committed to the cycle of preparation, repetition, and continuous improvement. Celebrate your success, but do not linger too long in the glory of past achievements. This journey is meant to be lived fully, an ongoing quest where each goal achieved sets the stage for the next.

With every preparation, every repetition, and every new challenge, you are not only moving closer to your dreams but also shaping the incredible story of your life. Embrace the journey, relish the struggles and victories, and always be ready for the exciting new chapters that lie ahead! Your aspirations are not just a destination. They are a lifelong adventure waiting for you to explore. As you finally catch sight of the shimmering City of Oz with its gleaming emerald facades, you may feel a rush of exhilaration. Yet even as we draw closer to this glittering metropolis, it often takes several more attempts before we can truly reach our destination.

And with each step forward, we begin to realize that perhaps Oz isn't quite what it was made out to be. Yes, there are emeralds, but beyond the surface glitz, we quickly find ourselves once more surrounded by a dense forest of challenges and obstacles. These transitional moments are what truly define us.

In the face of adversity, we have a choice to make. Do we transform into the cowardly lion and run away from what lies ahead, or do we dig deep and find the inner courage to continue pursuing our goals with tenacity and determination?

No matter how daunting the path may appear, you possess the necessary tools and resources to keep moving forward. Now is the time to implement those tools, embrace your potential, and repeat the process of striving toward greatness. Take action! Go out there, sign another declaration, click that registration button, or embark on your next significant dream.

It's crucial to recognize that as soon as that inner dialogue begins, wondering whether you should proceed or hesitate, you risk losing momentum, and your thoughts may start to drift in an uncertain direction. Remember, you are in control of the path your journey takes. You alone can decide whether you forge ahead or retreat into the shadows of doubt.

As you reflect on your accomplishments, appreciate everything you have achieved thus far, but always recognize the importance of returning to the grind. The journey doesn't end with one victory, nor does it pause for you to relish in your past successes. Instead, see it as an ongoing pursuit of the next Emerald City, your ultimate destination. Each goal you pursue is an opportunity to grow, learn, and expand your horizons.

Stay focused on what comes next, and acknowledge that every step you take toward achieving your dreams builds upon the work you've already put in. By maintaining this mindset, you create a cycle of continuous growth and improvement. Gather your strength, embrace the lessons learned from the challenges you've faced, and keep your eyes set firmly on the horizon. The road may not always be smooth, but with determination and a commitment to your vision, you will not only move closer to realizing your goals but also discover the extraordinary potential that lies within you. Get out there and chase that next adventure. Your version of the Emerald City awaits you!

STEP 2: NEW GOAL

In your journey, you have achieved something truly remarkable, and in doing so, you have redefined who you are. You took all the external and internal doubts that lingered in your mind and, with determination, buried them six feet deep in an unyielding casket, securely nailed down and bolted shut, leaving no room for escape. You accomplished something that neither you nor your closest friends believed you could do. You stepped up to a challenge that 80% or more of people in this world either can't or simply won't undertake. Now, as you bask in the glow of your achievements, it's time to set your sights on a new goal.

This is an exhilarating space to find yourself in, as you now possess firsthand knowledge of what it takes to achieve something significant. It's time for a recommitment to your journey. Consider the possibilities. Perhaps you just completed an Ironman or an ultra marathon. What can you possibly do next that will surpass that feat?

Your next goal doesn't have to be something as grand as swimming the Atlantic or running a marathon on the moon. Instead, choose something that resonates deeply with you and pursue it with a mindset of excellence. Strive to be exceptional in this next endeavor.

I recall a personal struggle as I faced this exact situation. After completing the Ironman challenge, I found myself trapped in the mindset that no subsequent achievement could ever compare to that milestone. I was looking at my next goal from the wrong perspective. In fact, it took me months to muster the courage to sign up for another event! Eventually, I committed to the Cleveland Half Marathon.

At the time, some people chuckled and pointed out that I was regressing in the level of difficulty. But for me, this wasn't about the challenge level of the event. It was about the internal battle I needed to conquer. I had to remind myself, with ferocity, that it was not about "Me vs. the Ironman" or "Me vs. the Cleveland Half Marathon." It was, and always will be, Me vs. Me.

This opportunity was my chance to build upon my previous experiences and to apply my new approach of Prep-Rep-Repeat. I aimed to surpass the expectations I had set for myself in earlier runs. I established a new standard and committed to upholding it.

In today's society, far too many people permit themselves to shy away from pressure, quickly fleeing from the next big thing that comes their way. But that's not how I operate, and it shouldn't be how you operate either if you are genuinely interested in uncovering your true potential. Raise the bar. Be the bar. You possess the capability to be the standard by which those around you will measure themselves. As you embark on this journey, remember that redefining your goals is a crucial part of personal growth. Allow yourself to embrace the process, knowing that each new challenge not only adds depth to your experiences but also equips you with vital skills that will serve you for years to come.

When you push through your limitations and continue to strive for excellence, you not only inspire yourself but also those who witness your journey. So, step confidently into the realm of possibilities, set your sights on that next goal, and cultivate the courage to strive for greatness. Your story is far from over. The next chapter is just beginning, waiting for you to write it with passion, persistence, and purpose. You have the strength within you. Now go and unleash it!

STEP 3: INSTILL A ROUTINE

It's time to return to the foundational elements of your journey and establish a solid base deeply rooted in the bedrock of life. Consider the Millennium Tower in San Francisco, which was built on unstable ground. The construction team worked tirelessly, digging and drilling to a depth of 800 feet, believing they had done enough to secure a strong foundation. Unfortunately, all too often, the idea of "far enough" simply isn't adequate. When we approach life with such a mentality, we run the risk of cutting corners. Instead of continuing to drill down another thousand feet to reach solid bedrock at 2,000 feet, they settled for a shallow embedment on an unstable sandy bottom.

Years later, the consequences became painfully clear. Not only was the Millennium Tower sinking deeper into the ground, but it was also swaying and tilting. The architect who designed the blueprint for this ambitious structure laid the groundwork and detailed the "how-to," but the construction company failed to follow through completely. They didn't tie their fundamental building blocks to a rock-solid base, and as a result, they are now faced with a significant and ongoing problem. The design may be revisited, and repairs may be made, but the integrity of the original structure will always be compromised.

As human beings, we are akin to architects of our own lives. It is imperative that we explore options that push beyond conventional plans. While following a traditional formula may yield results, it doesn't always account for the unique complexities and aspirations we each possess.

This is an opportunity to revise what you've laid out so you can enhance your life's work. Embark on some research, seek knowledge, and be willing to invest the time necessary to make decisions that align with your most profound dreams. This is also the perfect moment to assess and sharpen the areas of your life that may be lacking attention.

It's easy to lose sight of what's truly important when heavily focused on your personal goals. Never let your relationships, parenting, work, friendships, or other vital aspects of your life sink into unsteady ground for too long. If you neglect these foundational relationships, you may find they're no longer there to support you as you pursue your aspirations. Use this moment as a chance to refine your routine and ensure that all parts of your life are in harmony. In the grander scheme, if you can prioritize a holistic blueprint and tap into the countless possibilities that life has to offer, you will forge a stronger and more resilient structure.

Your life can become a masterpiece far superior to the Millennium Tower, one that stands tall and unwavering, despite the tests it may face. So, take the time to decide your approach. Plan your attack with diligence, and then execute it with conviction. Remember, every detail counts, and by laying a solid foundation, you are setting yourself up for success. Embrace the journey ahead with an open heart and a determined mind, knowing that every step taken is a building block toward the fulfilling life you are destined to lead.

STEP 4: TAKE ACTION

We've all been there, standing at the precipice of achievement, feeling the weight of our accomplishments while grappling with hesitance about the next step forward. This moment is simultaneously the simplest yet most challenging place to be, the edge between completing one goal and contemplating the pursuit of the next. It's essential to convince yourself that the time is now. This is game time!

Don't squander another second, because the truth is, the next second is never guaranteed. Take the intentions and declarations that you vocalize and transform them into tangible actions. Start by taking one step at a time. You might feel invincible, as though you're at the pinnacle of your game, immune to any threat of being dethroned. It's this very mindset that can lead to complacency and, ultimately, stagnation. We often charge forward, eager to leap into new ventures, only to stumble and fall flat on our faces.

The crucial lesson here is to remember that the goal for your first day in pursuit of your next big aspiration is simply to return and show up again for the second day. The objective of the second day? To keep the momentum going and come back for the third, and so forth. Avoid the temptation to overanalyze every detail of the new plan you've crafted. Instead, embrace this phase as the exhilarating part of the journey. You've already laid down the groundwork and committed to pursuing your goal with unyielding energy.

Now, it's time to honor that commitment and follow through on your promises to yourself. Understand that every significant achievement starts small. By focusing on consistent actions, regardless of how minor they may seem, you create a sustainable rhythm that builds momentum and strengthens your resolve. Each step you take is not just a move toward your ultimate goal. It is also a testament to your dedication and desire to grow.

Pursuing personal development and achievement is not

merely about reaching a finish line. It's about cultivating the discipline to keep pushing forward, even when it gets tough. Don't allow doubts or fears to derail your progress. Embrace the journey, relishing each day as an opportunity to move closer to your dreams. Channel your excitement and commitment into action, and watch as it transforms your aspirations into reality. You hold the power within you to propel yourself forward. Direction towards success and self-fulfillment is a choice you actively make. So, make that choice today, step up, take that leap, and remember that every great journey begins with a single step. Trust the process, stay persistent, and let your actions speak volumes about the future you are determined to create.

LIFE

In 2012, I reached a significant milestone in my life when I graduated from SUNY Brockport with a Bachelor's Degree in Physical Education. Entering the spring of 2013, I landed several substitute teaching positions at various schools, gaining valuable experience but still feeling uncertain about my long-term path. As summer approached quickly, I found myself at a crossroads, needing to make a firm decision about what to pursue next.

In June, my grandmother, Judy Barmore, mentioned that a small school, Sherman Central School, was hiring for a physical education position. Simultaneously, my college roommate shared that he had a solid chance of becoming the next PE teacher for the Sherman Wildcats.

Initially, I had no intention of applying for the position, convinced that my friend was all but locked in for the job based on his confident assertions. Days passed, and I began to hear from various people, including my high school football coach, who brought up the new opening repeatedly. Message after message, conversation after conversation, I slowly started to reconsider my options. Eventually, I was compelled to give it a shot.

In retrospect, it's clear that I should have recognized the signs sooner, but it took significant encouragement and self-reflection over several days to finally convince myself to fill out the application. In this crucial moment, I applied a four-step process to assess my current situation. First, I took stock of my circumstances and acknowledged the reality. I needed a job, and there was an opportunity right in front of me. This realization was both liberating and daunting. I had discovered the job opening on a Saturday, but the application deadline loomed just days away, falling on the following Wednesday. This sense of urgency pushed me to create a goal and formulate a plan in rapid speed. As I sat down to prepare my application, I reflected on the importance of seizing opportunities as they arise.

Life often presents us with crossroads; these pivotal moments can dictate the trajectory of our journeys. By choosing to act instead of remaining passive, I opened myself up to the possibility of new beginnings and exciting challenges. Embracing this new goal became a turning point. I learned that being proactive in pursuing opportunities is essential for personal and professional growth.

This lesson remains relevant today. Life rarely hands us success on a silver platter. Instead, we must be willing to step forward, embrace the uncertainty, and take the plunge even in the face of self-doubt. In your own life, when faced with similar crossroads, remember to assess your situation carefully and remain receptive to opportunities that may emerge, even when they seem to come from unexpected sources. Whether it's a job opening or a new project, don't hesitate to act.

Take the leap, apply the lessons learned from my experience, and commit to pursuing your dreams with determination. Ultimately, it's about fostering a mindset that welcomes change and challenges while building the courage to act decisively. So, as you navigate your own journey, don't shy away from opportunities that might feel daunting at first. Embrace them, and with each application, decision, or step you take, you carve out a path toward a fulfilled and meaningful life.

The very act of pursuing what you desire can illuminate a future filled with possibilities and achievements beyond what you initially imagined. My goal was clear. I wanted to position myself as an elite candidate, someone who would stand out from the crowd in a sea of applicants. The only routine I established for the following days centered around brainstorming every possible way I could present myself in the best light, maximizing my chances of getting hired. I constantly asked myself important questions: How would I differentiate myself?

What unique qualities could I showcase to ensure that I was chosen over the other 100 applicants vying for the same position? It was time to take action, decisive action. I refused to take the easy route of simply emailing my resume. After several days spent wrestling with nerves and overcoming my self-doubt, I chose to take a Tuesday off from my job and made the drive to the small town of Sherman to hand-deliver my resume.

I had only visited this rural community twice in my life, and despite its small size, it felt vast and unfamiliar to someone seeking to establish a career there. I arrived on a beautiful June morning, greeted by warm sunshine and the sweet sounds of nature. Upon entering the school, I was met by two kind women who were extremely courteous to this newcomer, a comforting gesture that eased my anxiety.

As I waited for ten minutes, a span that felt like an eternity, I mentally prepared myself for the meeting ahead. Finally, I had the opportunity to meet with the school principal, Mike Ginestre. When we sat down together, I introduced myself with confidence, maintaining eye contact as I offered him a firm handshake and presented my resume. We engaged in a brief but meaningful conversation, discussing my vision for the role and how my values aligned with the school's mission. As the conversation came to an end, I turned to exit the building, reflecting on the experience.

Throughout this encounter, I realized there is a right way and a wrong way to approach significant moments in our lives. While I may not have followed conventional protocols to the letter, I wholeheartedly believe that if you're going to do something, you should invest your energy and enthusiasm into that pursuit. Whether you are tying your shoes, submitting a job application, or training for an Ironman, the core principle remains: how you approach one task is a reflection of how you approach all tasks. This experience taught me the importance of commitment and passion in everything we do.

When we infuse our actions with genuine enthusiasm, we not only showcase our true selves but also pave a path to success. Remember that every challenge is an opportunity for growth, whether it involves pursuing a new job, tackling a fitness goal, or embarking on a life-changing adventure. So, as you strive toward your own aspirations, embody that spirit of energy and dedication. Commit to making your actions meaningful, and embrace the challenges that come your way with an open heart. By doing so, you'll not only enhance your personal journey but also inspire those around you to pursue their own dreams with the same passion and determination. Your journey is a culmination of the choices you make every day. Make each choice count, and watch how it transforms not only your path but also your entire life.

I was at a pivotal moment, one that had the potential to alter the trajectory of my life entirely. I was committed to not cutting any corners. I was ready to go all-in on my future. This was my chance to leave a lasting impression that would resonate with those around me. Fast forward a few weeks, and it must have worked because I landed the job. While many refer to it as "work," I viewed it as an opportunity to execute at a maximal level. At that time, I didn't fully comprehend the steps I was taking, nor did I consciously apply the "Prep-Rep-Repeat" technique in my approach.

Yet, in hindsight, I realize that this was precisely the mindset I adopted as I navigated this opportunity. Fast forward several years down the line, and I took immense pride in having created what I believe to be an elite physical education program. This journey also led me to form meaningful relationships and friendships while establishing a high level of expectation for my students to strive toward. I am not a guru or a master, just a simple educator, but I firmly believe that taking action with intention and striving for excellence in everything you do opens the door to extraordinary outcomes. It paves the way for unforeseen possibilities, such as "catching a break" or "getting lucky." Opportunities don't simply materialize out of thin air. They unfold as a result of persistence, diligence, and a commitment to performing at your highest potential.

Left: With my sister, Kari's last day at Sherman. It was so fun working alongside her for so many years. Right: Me and former student/athlete, Lucas Rater after we won the Sectional Championship for Football in 2019.
Barmore Photo Collection

UPDATE

I have since made, what I consider, another significant move in my career by resigning from Sherman Central School to pursue a path in personal training. Change can be both exhilarating and scary, but it is also a necessary part of growth. Not a day goes by that I don't think about the students and friendships I forged during my time at Sherman. That community will always hold a special place in my heart, and I will always regard it as my home. Go Wildcats!

As you consider your own journey, I encourage you to embrace the notion that every experience, every challenge you face, contributes to your growth and shapes your narrative. Each step you take is important, no matter how small. Consistency and perseverance are key components of success. Even when the path ahead seems unclear, trust in yourself and your ability to adapt and evolve. Embrace the power of resilience as you venture into new territories.

With each action, you are not just moving closer to your goals. You are also crafting a legacy that reflects your values, intentions, and the impact you've made on those around you. Life is filled with opportunities waiting to be seized. Take action, stay committed, and don't hesitate to aim higher. Your journey is not merely about reaching the destination. It's about who you become along the way. Embrace every facet of your experience, and let your story unfold!

IRONMAN

I dismounted from my bike and laced up my shoes, placing my headband on as I gazed down at the asphalt ahead. In the first ten miles, I felt prepared, easily passing the aid stations that offered Coca-Cola and pretzels. Having my family cheering me on every few miles was a tremendous boost for my morale. The course was divided into approximately five-mile loops, which became quite boring and monotonous. Seeing the same mile markers, houses, and familiar faces grew tedious, but I reminded myself that I didn't come this far to only come this far.

As I passed the Choptank River, the smell of saltwater and fish reminded me that I wasn't in Western New York; I was at the Maryland Ironman. Goosebumps covered my body each time I acknowledged that reality. With each step, I came closer to the 26.2-mile mark, but as I distanced myself from the start line, the miles grew increasingly challenging. I began stopping at the Coca-Cola stations, hoping the sugary drink would spark something my mind couldn't muster. It worked, and soon I found myself stopping at each station to refuel and reshape my beliefs.

Mile 23, then mile 24, and finally, mile 25 slipped behind me. It was then that I realized the past ten months had all boiled down to the final 1.2 miles ahead. Emotion surged within me as tears streamed down my face, and my pace quickened. Step by step, I could feel the end approaching. The last section of the marathon was mostly downhill, and I allowed the natural momentum to carry me toward the red carpet under the Ironman arch. I wanted to celebrate grandly as I crossed the finish line, but when Tony Lugo called out, "Brad Barmore, you are an Ironman," the only celebration I could muster was a fist bump.

I had done it. I was an Ironman. I was welcomed by my family and fellow athletes, transcending the title of a champion. I couldn't believe it, but as my wife hugged me and I held my son, I knew that every stroke, repetition, pedal, and step I had taken was worth it, especially on this end of the finish line. However, it was on the other side of that finish line that I encountered my most difficult challenge. One of the darkest periods of my life followed that weekend in Cambridge, Maryland.

One of the darkest periods in my life followed my

monumental Ironman experience. After training for ten grueling months, pouring my heart and soul into preparing for this single event, I found myself grappling with an overwhelming sense of emptiness once it was over. When you've been hyper-focused on a goal for such a prolonged period, it can be especially challenging to navigate the feelings of loneliness that often emerge after achieving it. This was a pivotal moment in my life, one that could have led me down two very different paths. I could have allowed myself to spiral out of control, choosing instead to pivot my focus toward a new challenge. But instead, I slipped into a dark abyss. It felt like being trapped in an expansive black room, void of light and hope, with no way out and no one to turn to for support.

Each day that passed felt heavier, and as much as I reached out for help, I found myself sinking deeper into despair. In those moments, I experienced a profound sense of solitude, unable to find the words or actions that might aid in my escape. I found myself engulfed in a profound fear, one that seeped into the very marrow of my being. I was frightened for myself, paralyzed by the uncertainty that loomed ahead.

The thought that I might never escape from this dark room of emptiness consumed me, filling my mind with doubt and despair. In those moments, the darkness felt suffocating, like a heavy blanket pressing down, making it difficult to breathe or think clearly. It was as if I were wandering aimlessly in a void, with no light to guide me and no clear path to follow. The walls of this metaphorical room seemed to close in on me, reflecting my internal turmoil and preventing me from seeing any glimmer of hope. Yet within this darkness, I began to realize that fear, though powerful, does not have to dictate my actions or define my reality. Instead of allowing myself to be immobilized by my apprehensions, I chose to confront them head-on.

I understood that acknowledging my fear was the first step toward liberation. In times of struggle, the uncertainty we feel can often magnify our challenges, making it all too easy to believe that escape is impossible. But in that moment of reflection, I learned the importance of resilience and the necessity of striving to illuminate the shadows surrounding me. With each breath, I took ownership of my fears and began to turn my attention toward the steps I could take, no matter how small. I understood that breaking free from that dark room would take time, effort, and an unwavering commitment to seek the light.

In every life journey, we will face moments when we feel lost and trapped in our own minds. We must recognize that these experiences do not define us. Instead, they challenge us to dig deep and uncover our inner strength. Just as one can only truly appreciate light after experiencing darkness, it is through moments of despair that we often find clarity and drive. So, as you confront your own dark rooms, remember that you possess the power to turn towards the light.

Every fear and obstacle can become an opportunity for growth if you are willing to engage with it. Embrace your journey, trust in your ability to overcome, and take those first courageous steps toward freedom. You may be surprised by how quickly the shadows begin to dissipate and how your newfound strength will lead you to a brighter, more fulfilling future.

Truly lost and not knowing what to do next. This picture sums up this period of my life. I was in the "darkness" reaching for a helping hand but not knowing what I truly wanted.
Barmore Photo Collection

Remember, you are capable of emerging from darkness and finding your way into the light. All it takes is the first step forward yet I couldn't get out of my own way. Days turned into weeks, and weeks into months, as I found myself drowning in a sea of mental anguish. Finally, I arrived at a crucial resolution. I had to redefine who I wanted to become. I resolved that my past accomplishments would no longer shackle me or hold me back from pursuing new goals. I was done reminiscing about my Ironman and ready to move forward.

With renewed purpose, I signed up for the Cleveland Half Marathon. Admittedly, this may have seemed like an underwhelming goal compared to my Ironman performance, but it signified the renewal of my ambition and the pursuit of something once again. There is no "only" in a half marathon, especially when your aim is to set a personal record. I returned to the drawing board, honestly assessing my current situation and acknowledging how the weight of my previous triumph was holding me back.

The urgency for finding new meaning consumed me. With my new goal in sight, I committed myself to achieving a personal record in Cleveland, Ohio, on Sunday, May 21, 2023. To do this, I instilled a new training routine, starting from the basics. Despite having previously conquered the distances of 2.4 miles for swimming, 112 miles for biking, and 26.2 miles for running, I knew my training plan called for a simple three-mile run on the first day.

Rather than letting my ego dictate my actions, I adhered firmly to my routine. This was an important lesson: returning to the fundamentals is essential if you want to achieve grand accolades. In this journey of self-discovery, don't grant your pride the power to dictate your actions or control who you are.

Avoid falling into the trap of thinking you know better than the routine designed to help you succeed. You have been in these situations before—trust the process, and focus on taking one day at a time. This approach is the only way to break free from the mental imprisonment that can arise from both past failures and, perhaps more importantly, past successes. As you embrace your journey, remember that each small, consistent effort contributes to your growth.

Cleveland Half Marathon. Got a PR that day. This was my "break through" that I desperately needed to break the "funk".
Barmore Photo Collection

Celebrate your achievements, learn from them, and then move forward. With each step you take on this new path, you are not only redefining your goals but also constructing a future filled with unlimited potential. So, dig deep, stay committed, and embark on this empowering journey with an open heart and a steadfast spirit. Your best days are ahead, and it's time to make your mark!

REFLECTION

1. You've recently completed a goal. What's next? How will you plan?

   _____

   _____

   _____

   _____

2. Have you ever done a long distance event? What was something that held you accountable during your training?

   _____

   _____

   _____

   _____

3. What is an occasion that you tried but failed? Did you give up or continue on?

   _____

   _____

   _____

CHAPTER 10

GRAND FINALE

You might wonder why my personal Ironman journey isn't the focal point of this book. The true essence lies not in the experience itself, but in the preparation for the Ironman and the invaluable insights that transformed my ordinary life into an Iron one. You may also notice that many chapters conclude with similar themes. It's a challenge to convey the importance of preparation, breaking through self-imposed limits, dreaming boldly, and taking decisive action in varied ways. However, I am committed to emphasizing these core messages and I hope with my endless persistence, they resonate with you somehow, someway. That's the sole reason I penned this book. I hope I can impact at least one person. As I wrap this up, I am filled with apprehension and fear at the thought of judgment or ridicule; however, the lessons I've gained along my journey compelled me to share my story. I realized I couldn't let fear silence my words.

I am nothing more than an ordinary guy who aspires for more. More from life, more from myself and that's really why I wanted to write this book. My journey has led me to seek out my true potential and to fully immerse myself in the experience of each day.

CHAPTER 10

For far too long, I felt like I was trapped on a hamster wheel, running in circles without making real progress. It wasn't until that pivotal "aha moment" in the Fall of 2020 that I began to see things differently. I discovered that every new day brings fresh opportunities, and you don't have to be superhuman. You simply need to be consistently committed.

I realized that I could finally step off that endless cycle and redefine who I had always wanted to be. Am I perfect? Absolutely not. I am far from flawless, but I am committed to making relentless attempts to be the best version of myself. It's a challenge we all face. Convincing ourselves that we are worthy of our dreams and aspirations.

We often become so consumed by the expectations of those around us that we lose sight of our true capabilities. The dreams we cherished as children can fade into the background, becoming distant memories. At some point, it's essential to sit down in silence and have an honest conversation with yourself. Ask yourself: Are you where you want to be? Is there more you wish to see, do, or accomplish? Are there dreams out there just beyond your reach that you wish you could grasp?

We all encounter breaking points in life, and while it may not be your fault that you find yourself where you are today, moving forward is your responsibility. Take full control of each day as though it were your last. Make the conscious choice to strive for your best self today. In this pursuit, aim for perfection. Now, perfection is a state free of flaws, a daunting ideal. While we can work diligently to reduce our shortcomings, achieving flawless perfection is, frankly, impossible. The journey toward perfection is ongoing and we will always be in pursuit of improvement. This relentless pursuit does not guarantee perfection, but it will lead you to a life that is undoubtedly fulfilling and rewarding and one that can be described as "pretty damn good."

Now is the time to get real with yourself. Look into the mirror and speak your truth. What is it that you have always wanted but have hesitated to chase due to fear or timidness? What dreams have you yearned for but lacked the courage to pursue? It's time to think BIG! Be bold in your aspirations.

Imagine beyond the confines of your current reality, and when you share those dreams with your closest friends, spouse, or siblings. If they laugh at you, that's when you know you're on the right track. GO GET IT!

This journey will take proper preparation, a substantial amount of repetition, and the willingness to engage in this cycle until you reach your finish line. You are fully equipped for this journey. You are the pilot of your own life. Now is the time to take control of your flight path, steering confidently toward the horizon as a champion. Trust in your abilities, lean into your dreams, and remember that every great achievement begins with the courage to take that first step. The adventure of a lifetime awaits you. Are you ready to embrace it?

QUOTES

What are your favorite quotes that you rely on for motivation?

1. _____

2. _____

3. _____

4. _____

5. _____

6. _____

7. _____

8. _____

9. _____

10. _____

"Our greatest glory is not in never failing, but in rising every time we fall."
- Confucius

ACKNOWLEDGMENTS

It would be inconceivable for me to have written this book, or to have accomplished anything remarkable, without the unwavering support of my wife, Adrienne. There's a popular saying: If you want to go fast, go alone; but if you want to go far, ensure you have a solid support system. Adrienne is that support system for me.

Barmore Photo Collection

She stands by my side, has my back, and leads the way in everything I pursue, both personally and professionally. Her presence has been and continues to be a shining beacon of positivity and encouragement in my life. No matter the challenge I face, Adrienne is always there, ready to help me transform my vision into reality. Her belief in my potential has fueled my ambition and strengthened my resolve, proving that with the right support, incredible things are possible. Always yours, Adrienne!! I love you.

To my beloved sons, Beckett Dean and Rush McKay, By the time you read this book, it will have been some years since I wrote it. You are both my "why"—the driving force behind everything I do. You are the reason I rise each morning filled with purpose and passion. You inspire me to chase ambitious dreams and to lead by example. The depth of meaning you bring to my life surpasses anything I ever could have anticipated. As I navigate through life, I often consider the ways I can inspire you, but in all honesty, it is you two who inspire me every single day to reach higher and strive harder.

Your enthusiasm for life and your generous hearts light up our world in extraordinary ways. I hope that I have been able to serve as a positive role model for you and that you both cherish the life we have built together. May you continue to embrace your passions with joy and courage, as you are my greatest motivation to always strive for more. Thank you for being the amazing individuals you are. Your love and spirit are my greatest accomplishments.

Barmore Photo Collection

To my dear Mom and Dad, our journey began with the three of us way back in the wonderful year of 1987. From the very start, you both served as the perfect role models for a young boy like me. You demonstrated the importance of hard work and passion, instilling in me the values that define a truly fulfilling life. I'm not sure I know five people who exhibit as much love and unwavering devotion to their family as you both do. You have set a remarkable standard for families, both near and far, to aspire to.

Thank you for always being my biggest supporters, no matter the event. Whether it was hockey, football, or our backyard rodeo, you were always front and center, cheering me on with boundless encouragement. I am deeply grateful for the exceptional tools you have equipped me with, enabling me to

191

grow into a man, a husband, and a father. Your guidance and love have shaped who I am today, and I cannot thank you enough for everything you have done for me. Your unwavering support is a foundational part of my journey, and I carry your lessons with me every step of the way.

Barmore Photo Collection

Brian, my youngest sibling and a tremendous source of inspiration in countless areas of life, I want to acknowledge the profound impact you've had on me. I genuinely believe that I would not have seen the bluer blues or the greener greens without you opening my eyes to the possibilities that life offers. You have exemplified the adventurous life I always aspired to live but never quite knew how to pursue. I recall vividly those moments when you were in your late teens, excitedly sharing with us your ambitious plans to travel the world with Kari.

Barmore Photo Collection

At the time, I couldn't help but laugh at the thought, but to my amazement, you not only voiced your dreams but also followed through with them. You showed me that it's not only acceptable to dream big, it's essential. When you completed your first half marathon, you redefined my perspective on challenges and what we are capable of achieving. Your determination inspired me to adapt and grow, allowing me to evolve into the person I am proud to be today.

I truly appreciate everything you have done for me, and I'm grateful for the loving, kind-hearted, and compassionate young man you have become. I often ponder where I would be in life without your influence and unwavering support. Thank you for being such a remarkable brother and for enriching my life in ways I cannot fully express. Your journey and accomplishments continue to motivate me to pursue my own dreams with the same vigor and passion you've exhibited.

Kari, my little sister, there was a time when it felt like it was you and me against the world. You've always been the brightest star on the block and the fiercest competitor in any arena. I fondly recall that unforgettable moment when you pulled my flag with your foot during a backyard flag football game. I vividly remember celebrating your achievements, such as scoring your 1,000th point in high school and being recognized as one of the Top 10 in free throw percentage in all of college basketball across the United States.

Barmore Photo Collection

Through these moments, you've demonstrated time and again that hard work truly pays off. But beyond your athletic prowess, you have taught me invaluable lessons about what it means to be a brother, a husband, and a father. Your unwavering support and insightful advice have come to me when I needed it the most, guiding me through life's challenges. Your zest for life and boundless enthusiasm are what so many people aspire to embody. I am incredibly proud to call you my sister, but even more significant is that I count you as a true friend. Thank you for being an inspiring force in my life and for showing me the beauty of hard work, perseverance, and authentic connection.

Nick Jackson, my friend and brother-in-law, you have been a guiding light in my life. Long before I fully grasped the concept of "growth," you offered me a glimpse, a small taste, of what it means to strive for more. My entire journey toward living an Iron Life was sparked by your recommendation to listen to the *MFCEO Project* with Andy Frisella. Engaging in conversations with you is always enjoyable. I cherish our discussions and the aspirations we share. Your vision closely aligns with the life I aspire to live, and I am grateful for the perspective you've brought into my world. Thank you for introducing me to opportunities I had not previously considered. Here's to many more years of inspiration and shared dreams! Cheers!

Barmore Photo Collection

To my boss, my cousin, my brother, and my friend, Jeffrey Witherspoon, I want to take a moment to express my heartfelt gratitude for the profound influence you have had on my life. There's a saying that you become what you surround yourself with, and your presence in my life has exemplified that truth. The exposure and guidance you have provided were exactly what I needed to navigate my journey toward fulfilling my true potential. You demonstrated that persistence truly pays off when paired with unwavering focus. Thank you for welcoming me into the E2M Family and giving me the opportunity to reconnect with the person I was always meant to become. Your support has been invaluable, and I am deeply appreciative of everything you have done for me.

Barmore Photo Collection

To Coach Tyrus Harper, I vividly recall the sense of intimidation I felt when I first met you in the summer of 2013. It was an eagerly awaited moment, and I am grateful for it to this day. Together, we spent several years in the trenches, where we learned invaluable lessons about patience, humility, and determination. Through our shared experiences, we cultivated the persistence needed to stand firm in our beliefs.

Barmore Photo Collection

I will always cherish the conversation we had in my office following the 2015-2016 season, where we boldly declared that one day we would win a State Championship. At that moment, it felt like a distant dream, but I never wavered in my faith or belief in you and your coaching philosophy. Your ability to demonstrate restraint during trying times has earned my deep respect and admiration. As you continue your coaching journey, I wish you nothing but the best. Individuals like you, who pave the way for young men and lead by example, deserve every success that comes your way. Here's to celebrating not just one, but three, four, and even five more State Championships in the future!

I want to express the utmost heartfelt gratitude and thanks to Charlie LaDuca. You were the catalyst behind the inspiration to not just write, but to take the bold step of publishing my first book and sending me to *simply francis publishing company*. Your impact over the years on and off the baseball field is easily one to emulate, and I am grateful for your support and our friendship.

I'd like to extend my heartfelt thanks to Rhonda and Frank Amoroso for transforming my words into a published work. You've made my dream of becoming a published author into a reality, and I am truly grateful!

Thank you for taking the time to read my self-development book about the trials and tribulations of training for an Ironman and the ups and downs of life. I hope that through my journey, you found inspiration and insights that resonate with your own experiences. Life is a continuous journey filled with challenges and triumphs, and it's my hope that this book serves as a reminder that resilience, determination, and a willingness to embrace the struggle can lead us to extraordinary places. Remember, every step you take, whether toward a race, a personal goal, or overcoming obstacles, is a testament to your strength and potential. Thank you for joining me on this journey, and I wish you all the best as you pursue your own remarkable adventures!

Barmore Photo Collection

IF YOU FEAR IT... CHASE IT!

ABOUT THE AUTHOR

When not writing, Bradley enjoys golfing, running, four-wheeling in the mud and spending time with his wife Adrienne, his sons Beckett and Rush and the rest of his family and friends. Bradley currently resides in Jamestown, New York and works virtually for a fitness/wellness company, E2M Fitness. When asked, *"What's your favorite adventure?"* The answer is always the same, "The next one."

Made in the USA
Las Vegas, NV
12 December 2024

13974026R00118